SOUTH WEST
SECRET
AGENTS

SOUTH WEST
SECRET
AGENTS

TRUE STORIES OF THE WEST COUNTRY AT WAR

LAURA QUIGLEY

For my parents, Rob and Carol.
They took me with them to see the world,
brought me up to appreciate the past and taught me
to recognise a great story. Thanks for all the adventures.

First published 2014

The History Press
The Mill, Brimscombe Port
Stroud, Gloucestershire, GL5 2QG
www.thehistorypress.co.uk

British Library Cataloguing in Publication Data.
A catalogue record for this book is available from the British Library.

ISBN 978 0 7509 5918 6

Typesetting and origination by The History Press
Printed in Great Britain

CONTENTS

IN MEMORIAM

When people tell stories of Britain from the Second World War, they often talk of 'the few'. I prefer to talk of 'the many' who risked and fought and laboured; if they had failed, there would be few of us left to write these stories. This book describes the lives of many who took part in secret operations, but there were many more, many who took those secrets to their graves, many who kept silent even after all the fighting was over. Of course sometimes there must be silence, but sometimes the world should be filled with the voices of the many.

Much of the activity of these stories is located in western Europe rather than in the south west itself, and I make no apologies for that – these stories are about the agents who brought people home and made the hazardous journeys back and forth across the Channel at a time when Europe was a fortress and at times when there seemed to be no hope of ever defeating the Nazis. And of course these stories are about the people who helped them.

At the outset, I would like to thank the following agents' relatives and friends who have contacted me to offer stories and photographs – I couldn't have done it without your incredible contributions. I just hope this book is a worthy tribute.

Dr Bruce Harris is associate professor in the Faculty of Medicine at Bond University in Queensland and the younger son of Flight Engineer Sergeant Charles 'Chas' William Harris, navigator of the 'Walrus L2312' seaplane (*see* Chapter 2). Sadly Dr Harris' elder brother Richard Harris died in the 1970s in a car accident, never knowing the facts behind their father's disappearance. Dr Harris is still investigating the Walrus' mission and has helped me with an astonishing amount of new information for which I am very grateful. For more on the Walrus' mission and her crew, please see Dr Bruce Harris' excellent website: www.walrus2014.com.

Alan Hall is researching and writing about the last mission of Walrus L2312 (*see* Chapter 2). I'm looking forward to reading his book coming out soon, with the working title: *Four Men And The Walrus*. Alan has generously corrected my work and contributed a great deal of new research to the case. Any mistakes in this book are definitely my own!

Access to the wartime diaries of Captain Cyril and Doris Wellington (*see* Chapter 5), along with related photographs, was kindly provided by their daughters Miss Ann Wellington and Mrs Margaret Gardner – brief diary excerpts have been quoted with their kind permission. If you would like to read the original diary entries, with extracts up until November 1942, they have generously given permission for it to be reproduced on the excellent website of the British Resistance Archive, researched and hosted by the Coleshill Auxiliary Research Team (CART). You can find the diary here: www.coleshillhouse.com/wartime-diaries-of-captain-cyril-and-doris-wellington.php.

Special thanks also to Nina Hannaford, one of CART's excellent researchers, for her invaluable work and for putting me in contact with Mrs Margaret Gardner who gave me even more wonderful information about her parents and their experiences. See the CART website for more fascinating details of all the Auxiliary Forces around Britain: www.coleshillhouse.com. If you have any more information about the Auxiliary Forces, please contact Nina Hannaford at cartdevon@gmail.com.

Philip Jarvis is the son of Pip Jarvis of the Inshore Patrol Flotilla (*see* Chapter 8). Philip not only shared with me the stories on his excellent website: www.adept-seo.co.uk/inshore-patrol-flotilla/ but also let me use the photographs. Again, any mistakes are definitely my own. Thanks also to Philip's family for their encouragement and support!

Sharon Lawn is the daughter of Jasper Lawn, coxswain of the N51, P11 and *L'Angèle-Rouge* (*see* Chapter 9). Sharon and her brother Raymond Lawn were very generous, sharing memories of their father, offering photos and correcting early drafts. Thanks to John Davies-Allen too for contacting me, offering resources – including the wonderful archives from www.islandrace.com (sadly no longer active) – and putting me in contact with Sharon and Raymond.

EXODUS

Maurice Southgate opened his eyes. He was in the water and the water was on fire. As he struggled to stay afloat, he realised the *Lancastria* was sinking and he wasn't alone out there in the open sea. Over 2,000 desperate survivors were in the water amongst the dismembered bodies, wreckage and burning fuel.

The naval port at Brest, France. (Author's collection)

The nearest French port, Saint-Nazaire, was over 5 miles away. England's south-west coast was 300 miles to the north, across the Breton peninsula and the English Channel. It was June 1940 and over 190,000 of the British Expeditionary Forces and their allies – French, Poles, Belgians – were still stranded in south-western France, gathered at the harbours around Brest and desperately awaiting the flotilla of ships sent from Plymouth, Falmouth and other British ports to rescue them.

Tens of thousands of them had previously waited at Dunkirk but the priority there had been to get the fighting men away, leaving signallers, mechanics, clerks and translators like Southgate to be harassed south by the relentless invading forces. Some 5,000 British servicemen were forced to surrender at Dieppe, surrounded by German tanks before the British evacuation fleet could reach them.

Every kind of ocean-going ship available was despatched to collect the remaining forces – trawlers, destroyers, ferries, cross-Channel steamers, French, Polish, Dutch and British, even cruise ships like the *Lancastria*, a British Cunard liner commandeered as a troop carrier for the war.

At La Pallice, the British officer in charge requisitioned local French merchant ships to get the British and Polish soldiers over to England. Across south-western France, 30,000 Polish troops were still fighting off the German advance as they made their way under fire to the ports, hoping to get to the boats in time. Meanwhile, three Isle of Man ferries rescued 6,000 from Brest Harbour, though their departure was delayed by German mines. The German tanks and land forces had not yet reached France's south-western shores but the Allied transports were already under constant attack by German submarines and the Luftwaffe. The Dunkirk evacuation further north was almost over, but Operation Aerial to evacuate the remaining Allied forces and refugees had barely begun.

On 17 June 1940, the *Lancastria* had just boarded over 5,200 troops and refugees, including women and children, brought out to her from Saint-Nazaire port in a frantic scurry of small boats. By 1 p.m., she was overcrowded with standing room only on the open decks. In fact, no one knows exactly how many were crammed on board that day – estimates range wildly from 5,000 to 9,000.

At 4 p.m., just as the ship received her orders to get underway, a German Junker JU-88 dive bomber made its run, targeting the *Lancastria*. The ships at Saint-Nazaire had been harassed by German air attacks all day but this time all four bombs hit their target.

One bomb exploded the *Lancastria*'s full fuel tank, spilling gallons of burning oil into the sea, while two bombs hit the holds. The fourth bomb plummeted down the ship's funnel, exploding in the engine room and blowing large holes in the hull. By 4.15 p.m., the ship was completely disabled and sinking.

Desperately trying to keep his head above the waves as he watched the ship roll and sink bow-first into the water, Southgate thought he could hear voices. Someone trapped on board the *Lancastria* was singing as the ship went down; maybe it was a group of them, all singing 'Roll Out the Barrel'. Others were bellowing out 'There'll Always be an England'. The voices carried across the open sea as over 3,000 people vanished beneath the waves in what remains Britain's worst ever maritime disaster.

If Southgate was one of the lucky ones, he didn't feel like it. He had to tread water for hours as the 2,477 survivors were gradually plucked out of the water and transferred to other troop ships. The *Oronsay* was already loaded at Saint-Nazaire but managed to take some of the bedraggled survivors. The *John Holt* took 829 and arrived in Plymouth on 18 June, followed by the *Cymbula* who had picked up 250 ragged troops and two female survivors.

But Maurice Southgate wasn't on any of these. Instead he found himself deposited in Falmouth on 19 June (probably by the *Prinses Josephine Charlotte, see* Chapter 2), two days after the sinking, with just a blanket and no shoes. An ambulance carried him to a makeshift camp where he simultaneously took a shower and lost his watch, then a coach reunited him with the remaining members of his squadron in the sergeants' mess at the Royal Air Force station in Plymouth.

Southgate had been working as a translator for the RAF in France. Though his parents were British, he was born in Paris in 1913, spoke fluent French, married a French woman and together they'd managed a furniture design business in Paris. This, however, was before the British declared war on Germany in September 1939. Now he was happy to be safely in Britain but he was also worried about his wife, alone in Paris.

As he downed beers in Plymouth with his friends, little did any of them realise that Southgate would be soon working with his wife again in France, as one of Britain's most successful secret agents for the Special Operations Executive. A saboteur? Who knew he had it in him?

Maurice Southgate had survived the sinking of the *Lancastria*, but could he survive the Gestapo?

Meanwhile, Squadron Leader Patrick Barlow was racing across France in a car, trying to catch the last British boat from Brest. He'd been in Nice on the eastern border working as a liaison officer for the French Air Force and, as the Germans advanced, Barlow was driving 400 miles across France in a last-ditch effort to get himself and his passengers back to Britain. The Nazi swastika was already flying from the Arc de Triomphe and Philippe Pétain, French military hero of the First World War, had just taken over as prime minister of the French Government and was discussing an armistice with the Germans to prevent further bloodshed. 'Vichy France' would soon be a reality. The political landscape of France was changing every minute as Barlow drove around the lines of refugees. Millions of French citizens, many of them all too aware of what they faced, were on the move, trying to get away from the advancing Germans with the few belongings they could carry. Along the road trudged women with prams, children, livestock, and old men pushing carts; all desperately trying to escape.

On the last leg of their journey to Brest, Barlow knew the German Army was less than 10 miles away. He drove on through the night, without lights, his passengers ready with machine guns in case they were stopped by a German patrol. They were lucky to make it to Brest Harbour, where they hurriedly boarded the *Lady of Mann* ferry.

As he clambered aboard, Barlow saw an old Frenchman with a *Légion d'honneur* rosette on his lapel forlornly watching them from the quayside. His elderly wife stood beside him, tears in her eyes, clutching their granddaughter between them. Like thousands of French civilians, they'd tried to board the evacuation ships but had been turned away.

'Are you British going?' the old lady cried out to Barlow, who mumbled an embarrassed response. It would haunt him for the rest of his life – the family he had to leave behind to suffer the German occupation. As the *Lady of Mann* docked at Plymouth at 4.50 a.m. on 17 June, Barlow was not alone in thinking he had to make it back to France some day – and soon. Thousands of the soldiers in retreat across the Channel were thinking the same thing, and hundreds of them would be making clandestine visits back to occupied France sooner than they ever imagined.

The French families weren't the only ones left behind. The British also had to leave their wounded. 'Walking wounded only,' was the disappointing response as the ambulance left Lieutenant Jimmy Langley of the Coldstream Guards on the beach at Dunkirk, still on his stretcher, just a few hundred yards from the evacuation point. He watched as the last ships left without him.

The Coldstream Guards had courageously defended the perimeter as the Germans attacked, losing 75 per cent of their own men but enabling tens of thousands of others to make it to the ships. However, when it came to Langley's turn, he was too wounded to go. The cottage he'd been using as cover had been hit by a German shell and the roof had collapsed on him. His left arm was a mangled mess that would soon have to be amputated and he was stuck on a stretcher that would have taken the place of four uninjured men on the departing ship.

The ambulance took him back into Dunkirk, to a large house serving as a hospital. He lay there worried that the Germans would shoot him: there were rumours that the Germans were taking no prisoners. But the first German officer he met saluted him and the German doctor safely amputated his left arm. Now he was a prisoner of war, hampered by his injury but still desperate to escape.

And escape he did. After many failed attempts, and a lengthy stay in a French prison, he eventually made it back to England to be appointed liaison officer between Britain's secret intelligence service MI6 and a newly formed group called MI9, organising the escape of prisoners of war, downed airmen and agents from occupied Europe.

On boats and planes from Gibraltar and Lisbon, heading into ports and airfields in Devon and Cornwall (primarily Falmouth, Plymouth and Dartmouth), there were over 10,000 such escapes during the Second World War.

From his little office in London, Jimmy Langley co-ordinated at least 3,000 of these, overcoming the many logistical problems of guiding them into south-west England with little, if any, additional help. Each and every successful escape was a personal triumph, with Langley worrying about the fate of each fugitive and the welfare of every agent he sent into Europe to help the escape lines.

After the war, hundreds of survivors would talk of the momentous day they were recruited or rescued by the one-armed man.

SAVING
ANNE DE GAULLE

Captain Norman Hope landed at Plymouth Roborough Airport on 17 June 1940. On paper, he was from the Naval Intelligence Directorate. In fact he was a member of the top secret Section D, established by the Foreign Office and MI6 in 1938 in response to the growing threat of Nazi Germany.

Hope's mission: to rescue the family of General de Gaulle, leader of the Free French Forces.

Section D worked closely with a secret research group studying the guerrilla war methods of Sinn Fein in Ireland and the effectiveness of sabotage against an enemy invader. By mid-1940, their clandestine operations were exploiting 'irregular' techniques on a scale never previously imagined. The list of their inventions reads like a James Bond script – the mass distribution of exploding German cigarettes being one of their more bizarre – and small incendiary devices were a speciality.

Before the war, Captain Hope had worked in Indochina and South America for the Asiatic Petroleum Company, a conglomerate of Shell and Royal Dutch Oil. Most of his colleagues in Section D were also non-military personnel, with backgrounds in law, industrial research and major corporations with contacts abroad. Some believe that Hope, who was fluent in French and Spanish, had a second secret mission – tasked not only with rescuing the de Gaulle family but with undertaking a visual reconnaissance of the fuel storage facilities at Brest, checking they had been completely destroyed by evacuating Allied Forces. The German military would need fuel after their rapid

Punch, September 29 1948

THE MAN MOUNTAIN
"The trouble is—can we keep him down?"

An old cartoon by Illingworth depicting Charles de Gaulle.
(*Punch*, 29 September 1948)

progress across France and effective demolition of the fuel reserves in France would delay a German invasion across the Channel.

As Charles de Gaulle established himself in London as head of the French in exile, the mission's priority was to rescue Madame de Gaulle and her children, still trapped in France under imminent threat of being captured by the Germans.

Charles de Gaulle in person. (Library of Congress, LC-USW33-019091-D)

To many during the Second World War, General de Gaulle seemed arrogant and rather aloof. In fact, British Intelligence was so worried about his personality that they paid Richmond Temple £300 a month to improve the general's public image. Even to his family, de Gaulle could seem distant and unemotional, showing affection only to his youngest daughter Anne, born with Down's Syndrome in 1928. Madame Yvonne de Gaulle was hit by a car just before Anne's birth in Germany, leaving Anne with injuries that left her unable to walk unaided for the duration of her life.

The family travelled a great deal during de Gaulle's career even before the war, living in Lebanon, Algiers and Germany, and Anne had always travelled with them, with a governess on hand to keep her safe. De Gaulle described her as 'my joy' and would read to her at bedtime and rock her to sleep.

While in Germany, the family quickly realised what 'eugenics' meant for their little girl; even in parts of France, there was growing support for the sterilisation of disabled people and the Nazis took the eugenics programme to horrific extremes. The de Gaulles understood the dangers of the fascists' ideology.

As France fell to the Nazis, French ministers discussed terms with the invaders, creating the fragile administrative zone of 'Vichy France'. But de Gaulle argued against working with the Nazis. At the time he was a relatively unknown French officer, new to politics, and few in the French leadership would heed his warnings. But his was a personal calling: his family were prime targets, so he contacted British Prime Minister Winston Churchill to negotiate a London-based French Government in exile. Churchill saw this dynamic, if sometimes discourteous, Frenchman as a powerful ally, giving hope for continuing Anglo-French resistance against Hitler's forces.

In June 1940, de Gaulle was travelling to an urgent meeting with Churchill, but at Bordeaux there were no aircraft available. Instead he made his way west by road to Brest Harbour where French destroyer the *Milan* was ready to take him to Plymouth.

On the way, he visited his dying mother one last time. He would never see her again. His wife, three children and Anne's nurse had already made it from the family home at Colombey-les-Deux-Églises to the then relative safety of an aunt's house on the shores of Carantec near Roscoff. As he boarded the *Milan* at Brest on 15 June 1940, de Gaulle arranged for an officer to deliver passports to his family. De Gaulle ensured that the French nuclear scientists, including Marie Curie's son-in-law, and their supply of 'heavy water', were also on the *Milan* heading to Plymouth – the history of atomic warfare might have been very different if the Nazis had captured these French scientists.

Philippe Pétain, prime minister of Vichy France.
(Library of Congress, LC-DIG-hec-21605)

The talks with Churchill went well and de Gaulle flew back to France the same day to discuss last-minute plans with the French Government, but the majority of French ministers were already decided on an armistice and Philippe Pétain was made prime minister. De Gaulle was now a 'marked man' and considered a traitor; faced with the threat of arrest by the French officials he made a daring escape to England on one of the few remaining planes not bombed at Bordeaux.

As they flew over the Breton peninsula, the countryside was on fire. At first de Gaulle thought the Germans were attacking, but in fact the remaining Allied Forces had set alight the British fuel storage facilities to prevent them from falling into German hands. Over La Pallice, de Gaulle witnessed a final horrific image of the fall of France – the French steamer *Champlain* with British soldiers on board had hit a German mine. He could see thousands of tiny figures struggling in the water. Her thirteen crewmen perished. The stricken ship was on her side, sinking to the seabed.

General de Gaulle escaped but he knew his family at Carantec were now in grave danger. The British tried to contact Madame de Gaulle to have her take the family to Brest, about 50 miles west, where they could be evacuated by a British destroyer. But suddenly all communications with Carantec were down. The Germans had arrived.

THE WALRUS

Carantec is an ancient village on the shores of Morlaix Bay, with wide sandy beaches at low tide. Only a seaplane would manage to reach the family and be large enough to carry the five passengers: Madame Yvonne de Gaulle, their children Philippe (19), Élisabeth (16) and Anne (12), as well as Anne's governess Marguerite Potel.

In Plymouth Sound, RAF Mount Batten was re-established as a seaplane base in the late 1920s. In 1940, the small Blackburn Sharks flying boats there had already evacuated men from Dunkirk. Also there was a Supermarine Walrus L2312 seaplane belonging to No. 15 Group Communications Flight, based at Roborough Airfield about 10 miles inland. The Walrus was exactly what Captain Hope was looking for. Now he just needed a crew.

Flight Lieutenant John 'Dinger' N. Bell, just 24 years old, was next on the duty roster and accepted the call, though he had no details of the actual mission until his 'secret passenger' Captain Hope arrived in Plymouth. A very experienced pilot, Bell had already flown a Walrus while in Australia and had successfully piloted Sunderland seaplanes into Brest, so was the perfect candidate. John Bell was from a family of three brothers from Farina in northern South Australia who had all volunteered to join the war effort in Britain. Farina, sadly, is now a ghost town and tragically only one of the three Bell brothers survived the war.

A Supermarine Walrus in the hangar. (Author's collection)

Flight Sergeant Charles 'Chas' William Harris (31) joined them as navigator. Harris had over 900 hours' experience successfully navigating aircraft across the Channel. He and Bell had already completed two missions together that month; they were a good team.

Both Bell and Harris were from No. 10 Squadron of the Royal Australian Air Force, stationed at RAF Mount Batten from April 1940. No. 10 Squadron was considered something special and were arguably the best Australian pilots in the war. Flying a Sunderland seaplane was an honour that came to very few but it was an honour earned and it certainly wasn't glamorous. In all weathers – and the weather in the Channel was atrocious – these pilots and their crews were constantly on patrol, hunting German submarines and on alert for air–sea rescues. For a sixteen-hour patrol over the Channel the Sunderland carried over 11,600 litres of fuel. They completed 42,951 flying hours, with dozens of enemy submarines destroyed and hundreds of Allied lives saved. The seaplanes of RAF Mount Batten and their courageous Australian crews flew further and more often than any other aircraft of the war.

Returning at night, the dark waters of Plymouth would be lit by rockets as the seaplanes descended, guided by this vivid flare-path. These flying machines were so massive – their wings 112 feet across, weighing 58,000 pounds when loaded – it took thirty ground crew to pull a Sunderland seaplane up the slipway and into the hangar at Mount Batten.

From the RAF came engineer Corporal Bernard Felix Nowell (25), an expert on the equipment. Nowell had some last-minute training on the machine gun and operating the radio set while airborne and managed some sleep for a few hours before they got ready to set off. Even the commanding officer of No. 10 Squadron didn't know where they were going or why – with their secret orders directly from Winston Churchill – but he knew they had the best team available.

On 18 June 1940, the Walrus, with Hope, Bell, Harris and Nowell aboard, took off from RAF Mount Batten at 2.55 in the morning, engines roaring across Plymouth Sound, the spray phosphorescent on the dark water. As the seaplane lifted into the clear night sky, Hope and the crew knew this was a dangerous mission into chaotic territory.

Walrus L2312 was never heard from again. The log entry simply states 'Failed to return'. Two days later, the Operations Record Book for No. 10 Squadron records the men as missing.

Later that same day, 18 June, de Gaulle made his first radio broadcasts from London, declaring: 'Whatever happens, the flame of the French resistance must not be extinguished and will not be extinguished.' There was still no word of his family. On 19 June, the Germans occupied the Brest peninsula, including Carantec, and General de Gaulle must have believed that his family was lost.

Short Sunderland V seaplanes. (Author's collection)

On 19 June a Belgian officer of the Royal Navy Volunteer Reserve (RNVR) named Van Riel, also from Section D, arrived in Plymouth to make another attempt to rescue de Gaulle's family and investigate the disappearance of the Walrus L2312. He assumed the rather unimaginative name 'Vann' for cover purposes and acquired a Motor Torpedo Boat (MTB 29), a new 70-foot Vosper commanded by Lieutenant C.A. ('Kit') James. They landed at Carantec at 6 a.m. on 20 June to discover the Germans had arrived just twenty-four hours before them, and there was no sign of Madame de Gaulle or her children.

German aircraft had already spotted MTB 29, so they had no time to explore the coast or gather more information. A quick return to Plymouth was their only option, but what had happened to the de Gaulles?

A LUCKY ESCAPE

On 17 June 1940, as news of the Germans' imminent arrival reached Carantec, Madame Yvonne de Gaulle travelled to Brest in a car driven by her sister. She visited the British vice-consulate to ask after her husband and discovered that the situation in Brest was dire. The Germans were approaching and the British were planning to blow up the navy yards, scuttle any remaining ships and destroy any fuel dumps to prevent them falling into enemy hands.

Brest Harbour. (Author's collection)

he destruction of the port was scheduled for 18 June 1940, Madame de Gaulle had no time to lose. Quickly, she returned to her children at Carantec, borrowed money from her aunt and they all headed back to Brest, driving through the night to catch the very last troop transport leaving in the morning of 18 June. She later described the nightmare of having to leave their luggage behind as they boarded the already overcrowded ship. By 11 a.m., German aircraft were bombing Brest, so it was a lucky escape.

In the chaos, it is difficult to identify which ship transported them across the English Channel, but only the journey of the Belgian *Prinses Josephine Charlotte* – a requisitioned Dover ferry – fits the known facts. She was 'picking up stragglers' from Brest Harbour at 8 a.m. on 18 June and was probably the last ship to leave before the demolition of Brest. She was then redirected to Saint-Nazaire to collect refugees there which means, by strange coincidence, *Josephine Charlotte* also probably brought home *Lancastria*-survivor Maurice Southgate (*see* Chapter 1).

Madame de Gaulle and her family safely arrived in Falmouth on 19 June 1940, ironically the same day that Vann and his MTB 29 had set sail from Plymouth to rescue them.

There's a story that Madame de Gaulle had a choice of two ships at Brest, one Polish, the other British, and she chose the British ship simply because of her husband's allegiance with Britain. This was fortunate as, it is said, the Polish ship was attacked and sunk on its way to Britain. In fact, the *Josephine Charlotte* was Belgian and Madame de Gaulle and her son both mention a Belgian crew in their accounts. The story goes that the Polish ship had already sailed before they arrived, but there's no evidence of such a ship. The only ship which had been at Brest and which was soon to be sunk was the *Meknes*. This ship left Brest in the early hours of 18 June, transporting 3,000 troops safely to Southampton, and was subsequently attacked and sunk by the Germans as it returned in July 1940 with French soldiers being repatriated to France (*see* Chapter 3). The *Meknes*, however, was a French ship and at no stage did it carry Polish crew (instead it was transporting French troops to Britain). Moreover, it was sunk on its return journey, not on its way to Britain.

Perhaps the story refers to the *Ulster Monarch*, part of a fleet of ships returning from a failed offensive in Norway and bringing French and Polish troops back into France as part of a last-minute effort to defend the country from German invasion. The *Ulster Monarch* arrived at Brest on 17 June, far too late for any major assault on the

German Army. Nonetheless the French troops decided to remain to fight in France while the 400 Polish troops elected to stay aboard, setting off for Falmouth around midnight on 17/18 June.

Or perhaps the 'Polish ship' was the *Sobieski* which had formed part of the same fleet as the *Ulster Monarch*. The *Sobieski* left Saint-Nazaire to the east of Brest in the early hours of 17 June 1940, carrying 2,890 troops and arriving safely in Plymouth. It may have dropped in at Brest on the way, possibly on 18 June, but there's no record of this. Also on 18 June, the trawler *Murmansk* was part of the minesweeping operations at Brest when she was grounded and the crew had to be rescued. Other than that, there seems to be no evidence of a Polish ship sunk en route to England, though many of the evacuation ships were attacked crossing the Channel.

In all the confusion, however, the British authorities seem unaware that Madame de Gaulle and her family were safe in Falmouth. Just after midnight on 25 June 1940, the commander-in-chief of the Western Approaches, based in Plymouth and organising the evacuations at that time, radioed the officer in charge of the last evacuation from Saint-Jean-de-Luz, France's southern-most port.

Liberation of Paris, 1945; note the banners in support of de Gaulle. (Library of Congress, LC-DIG-fsac-1a55001)

The commander was anxious to know if 'Colonel de Gaulle's party' had embarked at St Jean de Luz. Eight hours later they received the disheartening reply – all French parties had been refused permission to board the last ships because of the French armistice with Germany. The allegiance of French citizens could no longer be trusted.

They'd lost the family of Charles de Gaulle. All rescue missions, it seemed, had failed. It must have been a devastating blow, believing at that moment that General de Gaulle's family was likely in German hands.

However, Charles de Gaulle was better informed. On the 19 June, the entire Free French Forces comprised just two men – de Gaulle and his Lieutenant Geoffroy de Courcel – living in two rooms in a hotel in London. The telephone rang. De Courcel answered and was so overcome by the sound of the voice at the other end that he simply handed the phone over to de Gaulle. It was Yvonne de Gaulle calling her husband to say they'd arrived. They'd found rooms at the Landsdown Hotel in Falmouth but had had no idea where Charles de Gaulle was until their son Philippe spotted an account of his father's speech in an English newspaper.

Charles de Gaulle replied in typically stoic fashion, delighted but apparently unconcerned: 'Voila! There you are! Take the next train to London. I'll meet you at Paddington Station.' And at last they were joined by a third member of the Free French Forces – Philippe.

The Second World War may have been very different if de Gaulle had not had such particular affection for Anne, his youngest daughter. On 22 June, de Gaulle repeated his call to arms on BBC Radio: 'I call upon all Frenchmen who want to remain free to listen to my voice and follow me.' His cry of freedom was for her.

THE FATE OF THE WALRUS

So what happened to Walrus L2312 on 18 June 1940? It wasn't until 18 October 1941 that there was any news of the Walrus' crew. The War Organisation of the British Red Cross and the Order of St John of Jerusalem wrote a letter to the Air Ministry, saying they were caring for two young French boys who has escaped to England and told them the story of a crash they'd seen at 4 a.m. on 18 June. The boys had a number of ID tags and a visiting card belonging to Flight Lieutenant Bell.

Months later, a member of the French Resistance arrived in Britain carrying Captain Hope's wristwatch and some of his papers. Later still, the Red Cross found the graves of the four crewmen of the Walrus in the churchyard at Ploudaniel on the Brest peninsula, about 40 miles south west of Carantec, being carefully tended by local citizens. The graves of Bell, Nowell and Harris were clearly marked, but the fourth body was unidentified. All they'd found was a paper signed by a Sergeant Bennett at Mount Batten. Perhaps Norman Hope had been travelling under a false name.

Four men tragically died, that much is certain, and despite the Germans arriving at any moment, the French villagers still made the effort to retrieve the burnt bodies from the wreckage and bury them with honour. But the exact circumstances of their deaths are still unknown. There is one version of the story that, while trying to make the aerial survey of the fuel storage facilities near Brest before collecting the de Gaulle family, the Walrus became lost in fog and crash-landed. However, this was an experienced crew who knew the terrain well: John Bell was an excellent pilot and Harris an experienced navigator. They wouldn't have been lost or crashed in fog. Others say it was shot down by the French or the Germans, but all these stories have so far been discounted. Witness accounts deny the seaplane was damaged or on fire as she circled before coming in to land. To date, there appears to be no satisfactory explanation.

Another theory suggests that the Walrus hit a low embankment when it was trying to land in a field, but why would a seaplane be attempting to land beside the road to Brest when their destination was the harbour at Carantec? The de Gaulle family could provide no explanation.

Captain Louis Franck of Section D was first assigned to the Walrus mission, but at the last minute was sent urgently to Belgium instead and replaced by Norman Hope. One of Franck's favourite sayings was that 'Truth is far too precious a commodity to be used lightly'. The families of Norman Hope, John Bell, Charles Harris and Bernard Nowell are still searching for the truth.

But the men and their mission are not forgotten. Parts of the wreckage of Walrus L2312 were passed to the Australian War Memorial in 1980 by Flight Lieutenant Kevin Baff who was researching the history of No. 10 Squadron, and there's a plaque at Plymouth's Barbican commemorating the squadron's time at Mount Batten during the Second World War. In 2009, a replica of the Walrus L2312 was put on public display at the National Marine Aquarium in Plymouth (http://news.bbc.co.uk/1/hi/england/devon/7964767.stm) and the Walrus is still proudly displayed in Plymouth, on the pub's sign on Athenaeum Street.

Meanwhile, Australian researcher Alan Hall has a book about the mission coming out in 2014, with the working title *Four Men And The Walrus*. Families and researchers are still actively investigating the last hours of Hope, Bell, Nowell and Harris.

The mystery of the mission may never be solved, but the brave men of Walrus L2312 will certainly never be forgotten.

For more on the Walrus' mission and her crew, please see Bruce Harris' excellent website www.walrus2014.com. Dr Bruce Harris is the younger son of Flight Sergeant Charles 'Chas' William Harris, navigator of the Walrus L2312. His elder brother Richard Harris sadly died not knowing the truth behind their father's mission. Bruce Harris is still investigating their father's disappearance.

Norman Hope's nephew has also written a fascinating account of the mission, based on facts known at the time: www.bbc.co.uk/history/ww2peopleswar/stories/32/a2304532.shtml and David J. Smith, writer of Being Silent They Speak, *will include more about this mission in his next book.*

THE DEMOLITION OF BREST

Captain Hope had likely been tasked with surveying the oil storage depot at Brest, and his disappearance left British Intelligence with no news as to whether it was completely destroyed or had fallen into German hands. It was still a vital mission and the British Secret Intelligence Service (SIS) still had no viable agents in France. This state of affairs was partly the result of an agreement following the First World War, which stated that the United Kingdom would not locate any intelligence officers in French dominions, and partly because France had fallen so unexpectedly fast amidst the chaos of evacuation. The upshot was that information on the situation in France was sorely lacking and the British were left in the dark about enemy manoeuvres. Britain desperately needed to get agents into France to gather intelligence information.

The head of SIS quickly established a new section under Commander Kenneth Cohen of the Royal Navy. Cohen was tasked with working alongside the Free French Forces to get agents into France, not only to identify targets and report on the progress of the German invasion but also, as Vichy France became a reality in June 1940, to consider the mood and loyalties of the French people.

They were hampered by a lack of available transport. At the same time, Commander F.A. Slocum of the Royal Navy had been assigned a new section to re-establish transport operations into Europe, for the military and the intelligence services. Radio sets for agents' use were not available until the end of 1940, so in the summer of 1940 agents were expected to report back in person, but aircraft weren't yet available to drop and collect agents. Ships were their only option and Motor Torpedo Boats (MTBs) the fastest available.

On 20 June, a day after Vann's attempt to rescue the de Gaulles, a French MTB with an all-French crew, working for a temporary organisation called the Anglo-French Bureau, quietly landed an agent near Brest. The agent's brief was roughly the same as Captain Hope's: to report back on the state of the fuel storage depots and the navy yards and destroy anything that remained. Eleven days later, the same MTB returned and collected their spy. Sadly there is not much more information about this mission – the name of the first agent operational in France is lost to us, but this mission proved to be the first successful intelligence mission since the fall of France.

MOREAU
ON BOARD

The first Breton fishing boats arrived in June 1940. As the month progressed, more and more French sails were spotted bobbing up and down in the waters around Penzance, Falmouth, Looe, Plymouth, Salcombe, Dartmouth, and Brixham. Overladen with desperate villagers fleeing with their few belongings, these *barques de pêche*, some barely seaworthy, perilously crossed the Celtic Sea and the Channel to the relative calm of English ports. French civilians denied a place on the evacuation ships of Operation Aerial did not sit around waiting for the Germans.

Saint-Malo, fishermen out in their boats. (Author's collection)

Brixham, one of the port towns that saw the arrival of French refugees in 1940. (Library of Congress, LC-DIG-ppmsc-08054)

It was an extraordinary beginning to what would become a new era in British Intelligence. From these refugees, British and French agents returning to occupied France would be borrowing coats, cigarettes, cash, shoes, handbags, even bicycles and many other items that would assist in their 'disguise'. Unlike the German parachutist who landed in Britain in the wrong suit, with German sausage still in his pocket, the Allied agents would be able to blend into the French countryside – with a few unfortunate exceptions. The little details of French life these refugees brought with them became vital ammunition in the war against Nazi Germany.

Today these south-western harbours are the quiet domain of holidaymakers; it's difficult to imagine them bursting with refugees and evacuees from Europe in June 1940. One Falmouth resident declared that 'from the shore you could not see the horizon, so many boats were parked in the bay'.

Seven fishing boats headed for Penzance. The *Souvenir du Monde* sailed from Boulogne, with sixty-seven men, women and children aboard. The *Corbeau* fled Carmaret with just nineteen. Seven more small vessels carried 350 people; whole villages escaping to the sea. By 23 June, 5,500 refugees had landed at Falmouth. A Boulogne boat arrived in Brixham Bay carrying seventy passengers, all named Duval. The flotillas appeared in every major port from Penzance to Portsmouth.

Centuries before, as the Saxon hordes invaded England, the desperate Britons of south-west England escaped to their boats and to France. The two coastlines subsequently shared a long maritime history with decades of raids and warfare, fishing and smuggling. Now the fleeing Bretons were returning to England as yet another brutal force drove them back across the Channel. Soon these same boats would be smuggling people and explosives back to the French coast.

On 18 June 1940, the Channel Island ferry *St Helier* left Plymouth at 10.35 p.m. for La Pallice, to assist with Operation Aerial. En route the captain was astounded to pass yet another flotilla of assorted French ships dashing for English ports. Between 19 and 26 June, Plymouth would receive more than thirty French ships carrying civilians as well as servicemen. The *Strathaird* arrived with 6,000 troops, hundreds of civilians, 200 children and the gold from British banks in Paris. The *Aresthusa* brought the President of Poland and 250 British embassy staff from Brussels and Paris. On 22 June, the troopship *Ettrick* left Saint-Nazaire with 2,000 civilians, including the king and queen of Albania and the Albanian crown jewels, and the *Alderpool* arrived carrying around 2,800 Polish troops and seventy refugees after a desperate voyage across the Channel with no food and water on board. As the refugees arrived, there were harrowing scenes in the English harbours.

53   LA PALLICE-ROCHELLE. — Quatre-Mâts sortant du Port. — LL.

La Pallice-Rochelle, the destination for Channel Island ferry *St Helier.* (Author's collection)

On 24 June 1940, the *Beagle* reported she would soon be arriving at Plymouth in the early hours of 25 June carrying naval personnel, demolition stores, one 'stretcher case', one wounded officer, one 'doubtful escaped British prisoner', two Germans and three ladies – all of whom would require identification. Security was going to be a problem.

Dunkirk and Operation Aerial should have demoralised Britain, but the stoic resolve of the evacuees was contagious. Of course, there was also the bloody-minded resolve of the British. Flying Officer Frank Brinsdon described the mood in Fighter Command in July 1940: 'We were absolutely confident that we were better than the enemy, and wanted an opportunity to bloody Hitler's nose.'

General de Gaulle praised the flotilla that arrived in the last days of June 1940, bringing to the Free French Forces hundreds of able-bodied men from the Île de Sein. These were the lucky ones – under the Nazis the Île de Sein became virtually a prison camp for women and children while any men who remained were carted off to fight for Germany.

The British had expected the fight against the Nazis to take place on the European mainland, not across a siege line along southern Britain. Reconnaissance missions and trained saboteurs were suddenly more necessary than ever and before long many of the refugees would be taking part in clandestine missions back across the Channel.

Hubert Moreau was one of the first.

ESCAPE FROM CONCARNEAU

A cavalry cadet and son of a French vice-admiral, Hubert Moreau had been captured and imprisoned by the Germans at Lorient in southern Brittany. As the prisoners were moved, however, Moreau managed to escape. With the encouragement of the parish priest and the family Gauchard at Concarneau, Moreau and his distant cousin Gérard stole a 4-metre open boat *L'Albatros* from the beach at Beg-Meil – a boat completely unsuited to crossing the Channel. The pair spent a wretched week making their way to England.

On 1 July 1940, the policeman at Polperro in Cornwall was called to the quayside to discover two ragged individuals had arrived in a battered French boat. Moreau's cousin was so seasick and malnourished he could neither speak nor stand. Unsure of what to do, the policeman duly questioned them in case they were spies – peering down over the

The beach at Concarneau. (Author's collection)

pier at the pair caught in the mud of low tide, he asked if their passports were appropriately endorsed by the British consulate. Moreau politely replied that his passport was unfortunately still in Paris.

Humanity prevailed and Moreau was happily escorted through the picturesque village by the local schoolchildren, filling his pockets with chocolate and cigarettes, while Gérard followed carried on a stretcher that was rapidly filling up with gifts of oranges. Moreau describes the scene as like something from a movie. With his film-star good looks and exciting escapades, Moreau quickly became a local celebrity.

Moreau and his cousin certainly fared better than some of the refugees. News reached Britain that the French were co-operating with the Nazis and many French crews were forced to remain on board their boats until the British authorities had 'cleared' them. At Penzance, the families were permitted ashore, but the crews remained aboard as captives. The French boats were left in the harbour likely to be sunk by the Royal Navy if they attempted to set sail, but the crews were starving, and the local representative of the French consulate was forced to find £400 to supply them with food.

The fall of France made the English afraid of their former allies. Now the French Government under Pétain was negotiating a sort of peace with the Nazis, creating 'Vichy France' – could the French be trusted? Many French initially supported the Vichy agreements, saving France from further bloodshed, but that did not necessarily make them pro-German or anti-British.

Polperro Harbour. (Photo by William Fathers of Polperro News, www.polperronews.com, and reproduced with his kind permission)

French refugees in Britain, however, were forced to choose on arrival. If you wished to remain in Britain you had to choose to fight for General de Gaulle, but to many French nationals de Gaulle was an unknown quantity. Many did not take to his aristocratic airs or his opposition to the great French hero of the First World War Pétain, now head of the Vichy Government. The Vichy consulate still operated in Britain, irritated by de Gaulle's establishment of an alternative French Government based in London. Those refugees, French soldiers and officials who chose to support the Vichy Government's armistice were interned in camps and repatriated as potential enemies of Britain.

Mistrust developed on both sides. Refugees arrived to false rumours that suspected French spies had been shot. At the same time, all arrivals were interrogated by MI5, Britain's home security organisation. Although the interrogations gave British secret services invaluable information, many refugees were distrustful of their motives. Perhaps it is unsurprising, then, that a number of French citizens arriving in the West Country were described by one observer as profoundly pessimistic, believing that even the food offered by local authorities was merely a publicity stunt. Meanwhile, French women in Cornwall refused to work in the munitions factories – on bombs that would soon be falling on French targets – and they protested about the living conditions, many having to be housed in old prisons.

Worried that the French fleet at Mel-el-Kébir in Algeria might fall into German hands, Churchill ordered a bombing raid on 3 July 1940 that killed 1,200 French sailors. In the same operation, 130 French ships lying in British ports were boarded out of concern that they might suddenly ally themselves with the Germans. The British, who also seized control of the French naval codes, seemed to be declaring war on the French. Had Moreau and his cousin escaped France only to be shot by the British?

In May 1940, the French submarine *Surcouf* found herself being refitted in Brest under threat of attack by the Germans, and, with a jammed rudder and only one engine working, she limped into Plymouth to escape. The *Surcouf* was the largest vessel of its type in the world – potentially a great asset to the Free French Forces, but the crew had no time for the overtures of de Gaulle. On 3 July, the *Surcouf* was boarded by the British. The *Surcouf*'s crew fought back and two Royal Navy officers and a French engine room officer

Penzance. French families arriving here might be allowed ashore but members of the crew had to remain in their boats until they were 'cleared' to enter Britain. (Library of Congress, LC-DIG-ppmsc-08233)

were mortally wounded in the skirmish. A British seaman was shot dead by the submarine's doctor and three French were wounded as their shipmates were dragged into prison.

Nearly 1,300 captured French soldiers were repatriated to France aboard the liner *Meknes*, sailing from Southampton, only for the ship to be sunk by a German torpedo with 300 lives lost. Survivors, many pulled out of the water half-naked and wounded, were billeted in Plymouth, Portsmouth and Skegness. The French blamed the British for the tragedy, for failing to negotiate the repatriation with the Germans. These events did nothing to alleviate the growing mistrust between the former allies.

A MAD HOUSE

In the midst of this chaos and resentment, Hubert Moreau and his companion arrived in Polperro and were transferred to Plymouth for questioning. They spent their first afternoon in Plymouth in what Moreau describes as a lunatic asylum. It's likely they were housed in Ward K of the Royal Naval Hospital in Stonehouse, where mentally ill patients were kept; this would have been the ideal location to keep them away from serving officers and yet offer them the medical attention they needed.

It was a strange interrogation. It didn't take long for the navy intelligence officer to realise that Hubert Moreau and Gérard were not German spies and the two soon found themselves in a military car heading for the pub: a true Plymouth welcome. Fatigue and alcohol meant that Moreau could not remember much of the afternoon until 'resurfacing' for dinner at a very posh hotel at the invitation of their interrogator, whose charming French wife knew Moreau's family by coincidence. But the discussion at the dinner table soon became serious – the British were desperate for information about the situation in France at the time of Moreau's hasty departure.

'It would be very interesting if you could tell me exactly what happened in France at the time of your departure. We completely lack information on the current situation,' their host explained, 'and I know that up-to-date information would be very much appreciated in London. It would be really useful to be able to follow from day to day what the Germans are doing in occupied France.' In fact, British Intelligence lacked even up-to-date maps of France.

So a return to France was on the cards and Moreau accepted the challenge. Here was just the kind of undercover agent the British were looking for: trustworthy, reliable, with military experience and a good knowledge of the territory.

Moreau was directed to the British Secret Intelligence Services (SIS) in London. Gérard was still recovering from their ordeal, so went to stay with relatives while Moreau dined alone at the Rubens Hotel near SIS headquarters in London, with the waiter silently disapproving of his presence – Moreau still looked like a 'hobo'.

It was here that Moreau experienced one of life's strange coincidences. Two French officers staying at the hotel entered the dining room and Moreau, despite his dishevelled appearance, went over to introduce himself. One officer he recognised, Lieutenant de Courcel, but the other was unknown to him. Moreau had unwittingly just introduced himself to the new leader of the Free French Forces, General Charles de Gaulle.

De Gaulle was delighted with Moreau's mission for British Intelligence and asked to be kept informed, recruiting Moreau to the Free French Forces. Moreau was offered a choice of transport into France – boat or parachute. The idea of landing in France by parachute without a reception committee filled Moreau with horror, so boat it would have to be, and (considering the tensions between the British and the mainland French and the dangers of crossing the Channel) Moreau realised his best chance of returning to France was the way he had come – by fishing boat.

HEADING HOME

He needed a crew, ideally people who knew the Brittany coastline, and a suitable ship. Many of the Breton fishermen had been forced to report to the London officials and were being 'accommodated' in the Olympia exhibition hall. Moreau was introduced to a group of Bretons morosely congregating in a corner, probably wondering why they had escaped one authoritarian regime only to be imprisoned by another.

Among them was a 19-year-old boy called Raymond le Corre, a solid and obstinate lad who Moreau liked on sight. Raymond had escaped by boat from Le-Guilvinec, coincidentally not far from Moreau's escape route via Concarneau. After the Germans had invaded his home, Raymond and his friends had stolen away aboard an old sardine pinnace, the *Korrigan*, to Mevagissey in Cornwall, arriving on 27 June 1940. The *Korrigan* was one of the very first recorded civilian escapes from German occupied territory. Surprisingly, considering that the German Army was entrenched along the French coast, there would be many more.

Moreau and his new recruit arrived in Falmouth on 10 July 1940, looking for a suitable vessel. Their first choice was a cutter-rigged crabber the *Rouanez-ar-Peoc'h* or the '*Queen of Peace*'. The ship had arrived on 24 June from the Île de Sein carrying thirty-five refugees. The five Breton crewmen immediately volunteered for the mission, but Moreau changed his mind when he learned that these men had twenty-six children between them, left behind on the Île de Sein. Sympathetic to their desire to return to France, he couldn't bring himself to risk their lives or put their families in more danger.

Moreau's second choice was a sardine pinnace from Douarnenez in Brittany. The 52-foot ship had been requisitioned by the French Navy but was slowly sinking in Falmouth Harbour, her engines under water due to a small leak. Le Corre and an engineer from the Royal Navy base at Falmouth supervised repairs while Moreau set out to find a crew.

As July 1940 began, the Luftwaffe was already bombing south-west ports in preparations for the coming invasion. On 5 July, Falmouth and Torpoint were hit and Plymouth was bombed the following day, killing three civilians.

Portsmouth was first hit on 11 July. In the harbour there sat an old battleship, the *Courbet*, once the pride of the French Navy, now stuck without power. Manned by French fishermen, it was being used as a floating anti-aircraft battery, defending Portsmouth against the Luftwaffe attacks. Amongst the crew, Moreau discovered three of Le Corre's old travelling companions – Le Goff, Baltas and Guénolé from Le-Guilvinec – and immediately signed them up for the mission.

British Intelligence had established a second section under Commander Wilfred Dunderdale to get agents into France, but mysteriously the Free French Forces were not involved (or perhaps not so mysteriously as British Intelligence still weren't sure about trusting the French). Obviously they were keeping their options open. Ironically, it was Hubert Moreau working for the Free French who would be Dunderdale's first agent in France; there was no one else so readily available and suitable for the mission.

Portsmouth Harbour, in which the *Courbet* would have sat waiting to protect the city from enemy aircraft. Portsmouth would endure some seventy air raids between 1940 and 1944. (Library of Congress, LC-DIG-ppmsc-08800)

To help Moreau, Dunderdale sent his assistant, a 6-foot-6 Irishman affectionately nicknamed 'Uncle Tom' Greene. It's likely Uncle Tom was also there to investigate the potential for a secret flotilla base in the Falmouth estuaries. By the end of August 1940, Dunderdale would establish the Mylor Flotilla of fishing boats for the transport of agents to France, operating from Mylor Creek off Falmouth Harbour. Moreau's venture was the first of many.

Moreau's ship was now ready and the eager crew decided to call it *Le Petit Marcel*. Then the allocated British rations arrived and their faces fell. Moreau and Uncle Tom hurriedly set out for more appealing supplies, returning with a barrel of Algerian red wine, French bully beef and French biscuits. What the Royal Naval base thought of the new rations is left unrecorded by history, but the military disdainfully viewed these early clandestine voyages as the work of amateurs.

Finally, on 26 July 1940, they were ready and set sail at 4 p.m., waved off by a tearful Uncle Tom. However, the Contraband Control Service had received no instructions about the departure and the secret mission was stopped at the entrance to Falmouth Harbour. Suddenly the mission could not remain quite so secret, as Moreau had to produce a letter from the local navy officer calling on all British naval authorities to give *Le Petit Marcel* every aid and protection. Even clandestine operations required permits.

At last they were crossing the Channel. It was an emotional moment for them all. However, they knew so little of the situation at their destination: so much had changed in just a few months. Which of their former friends and associates could they trust? What news would they get of their families? Slocum's powerful MTBs were struggling to get other intelligence agents into mainland Europe – one MTB arrived successfully at Saint Pabu on the Brest peninsula, only for the agent to refuse point-blank to disembark. It was too dangerous. Meanwhile, Moreau's little crew of Breton fishermen on their repaired fishing boat had one significant advantage: they were heading home.

THE HOME FRONT

On 28 June 1940, the residents of Plymouth suffered their first air-raid alert. On 5 July 1940, the first high-explosive bombs hit Charlestown near St Austell with nine people injured. Then bombs fell on Falmouth Docks at 4.15 p.m., and at 4.20 p.m. one of the oil tanks at Torpoint exploded. Cornwall, it should be remembered, still had no public air-raid shelters. Back in Plymouth, the first bomb hit on 6 July 1940, destroying houses on Swilly Road in Devonport and killing three people.

These were the first attacks by the Luftwaffe on southern English ports. During July and August, hundreds of bombs fell across Devon and Cornwall, a strange scattering of targets that show how ill-planned these early raids were. The targets, moreover, weren't just military – Millbrook was machine-gunned and farms around Fowey caught fire. One bizarre bombing attack dropped sixty-five bombs and scores of incendiaries along a parabolic path across St Austell, Carthew, St Breock, St Issey, Colan, Carharrack and Falmouth, completely missing the intended target of the vital St Eval airbase near Newquay. France had fallen and, as the Battle of Britain filled the skies, the German Forces were now focusing their attention on the invasion of Britain.

Barbed-wire barriers were swiftly erected across the north of Plymouth and roads were heavily guarded. The Germans, it was generally believed, would land somewhere east of Plymouth and attempt to take the port from the north. Patrols were out across Dartmoor looking for German parachutists, and the Women's Voluntary Service set out daily on horseback, patrolling Dartmoor, binoculars ready to spot any sign of early invaders.

The Luftwaffe dropped magnetic mines around Plymouth Sound, creating chaos for ships and the seaplanes on the Cattewater at RAF Mount Batten. Each day minesweepers cleared the seas so the British Forces could access their own harbours.

While the battles were consuming the skies, everyone on the ground was preparing for an invasion.

SECRET LISTENERS

So what did the people of the south west think about all this? That, in fact, is exactly what the government wanted to know and they employed a new agency of spies to eavesdrop on the conversations and behaviour of the British people.

Mass Observation was founded in 1937 by three men: a social anthropologist, a poet and the documentary film-maker Humphrey Jennings, who would later produce the films *Fires Were Started* and *Listen to Britain*, documenting the everyday lives of the British surviving the Blitz.

At the outset it was just anthropological research – documenting the moods and behaviour of people, initially amongst the factory workers in Bolton, but Mass Observation employed a range of rather unorthodox techniques for assessing popular attitudes. The people didn't know they were being recorded. It was literally eavesdropping – not so bad if the aims are just peaceful research, but add a world war and some politicians and you've got a secret police force monitoring everyone and making daily reports to the Home Intelligence department of the Ministry of Information.

On 11 July 1940, the Ministry of Information, headed by Alfred Duff Cooper, launched a major radio and poster campaign warning of the dangers of repeating rumours. People were encouraged to join the 'Silent Column' and report to the police anyone saying anything indiscreet.

Suddenly there were a flurry of arrests of people who'd been overheard making disparaging remarks about British leadership. The result was a public outcry against 'Cooper's Snoopers', all the more vitriolic when the press reported details of the Ministry's doorstep campaigns and surveys to 'investigate public morale'.

The people of the south west were alarmed and annoyed by such spying – they felt it was an attack on the freedom of the individual to speak their mind:

'Of course I think rumour's a bad thing but I find myself defending it now that people are being prosecuted.'

'I feel really angry. It's the Gestapo over here.'

'They can prevent us talking but they can't prevent us thinking.'

If they couldn't criticise their own leadership, then what were they fighting for? It was a very British battle, for the right to 'have a moan' if they felt like it.

In pre-war Germany, when church pastors criticised the Nazis, Hitler had 800 of them brutally rounded up and sent to prisons, so the British Government's response was in contrast more benign. Instead, Secret Regional Information Officers could often be found sitting in the pub or chatting informally to friends at work, quietly taking notes which would be telephoned through daily to Bristol, then transmitted to London and collated into daily briefing papers for senior ministers. One secret observer in Plymouth reported on public morale after each air raid, based on the number of items hanging on the high washing lines that characterise Plymouth's terraced houses.

The reports lasted unabated until September 1940 – they would inform speeches, policy and the wording of news items. Churchill himself was listening in. On a daily basis they were not the most accurate gauge of public opinion, but read as a long-term study, they reveal astonishing fortitude and a British people determined to fight against all manifestations of fascist behaviour, at home or abroad.

In 1940, there were rumours of German sabotage throughout the south west and local upsets, such as the water mains bursting in Exeter in May 1940, were blamed on the enemy. Every week there were more false stories of German parachutists landing in Dartmoor or Germans disguised as nuns travelling on British trains. There were even rumours that Hermann Göring, head of the Luftwaffe, had parachuted into Plymouth and had been seen personally inspecting the damage.

When Vichy France was established, there was general criticism of Pétain but overwhelming sympathy for the French people. Churchill's recognition of General de Gaulle as leader of the Free French did much to stabilise British concerns about the French situation.

Refugees were seen a security risk; often the only security checks were done by the village police constable and the harbour master. The public thought that spies or 'Fifth Columnists' – a term

borrowed from the Spanish Civil War to denote a subversive organisation seeking to harm the country – were everywhere. However,
racist attacks were surprisingly few. When Italy declared war, there
was one attack on an Italian café in Exeter but this was considered
the work of hooligans and locally abhorred.

Bristol reported the 'suspect activities' of the Cotswold Bruderhof.
This Christian pacifist community, based on the border between
Gloucester and Wiltshire, had escaped extreme Nazi persecution
when they were given forty-eight hours by the Nazi authorities
to get out, and in 1938 they settled in England. As war broke out,
their anti-war stance attracted many British conscientious objectors, swelling their numbers to 350 living on an old-fashioned farm,
rather like the Amish. Their pacifism attracted suspicion and in
1942 the British authorities confronted them with an ultimatum –
all German members would either be interned or leave England as a
group. The group chose to leave England and managed to find some
acceptance in Paraguay.

Faced with invasion by the Germans, there were attacks on the
British Government for its 'muddling unpreparedness' and the lack
of jobs for those eager to contribute to the war effort. They also
wanted to hear the real news with detailed casualty lists, no matter
how bad it was, rather than upbeat propaganda.

Exeter, first bombed in August 1940. (Library of Congress, LC-DIG-ppmsc-08366)

In the south west it was generally believed that Hitler's invasion of England would start on 1 July 1940 and all be over by mid-August. The secret eavesdroppers reported that the public were happy to build anti-tank trenches to repel the invaders. Nancy Bazin was in the civilian force mobilised to defend Exmouth and she tells a slightly different story:

> We were told that we had to mobilize all our civilian force in Exmouth to resist the invasion that was likely to come across the Channel. Our local battalion of Devons which were organising this were going round with microphones and loudspeakers, calling us to come to the beach with spades and shovels, anything we could lay our hands on. And I had several friends, I remember particularly the stretch of sand allotted, it was very near to where our lifeboat station was. We were told to dig and we dug a trench in the sand … At the same time as digging, and getting blisters on our hands, and working for hours in this, we were looking out to sea expecting to see these flotillas of German invading troops come. On this whole two-mile stretch we were digging this trench and it was absolutely hopeless because, with the wind and the rain and the high tide, all our work would disappear. But we did it, in this extraordinary way, believing that somehow we were defending. That was a futile operation. There was a sergeant or an officer every hundred yards saying, 'Keep digging'.

As the first bombs dropped on the south west, there was severe criticism of the lack of defences, particularly in Newquay and Exeter. Even the better-fortified Plymouth had problems with the sirens and there weren't enough fighter aircraft to defend the region. By July/August 1940 the Gloucester Gladiator biplanes at RAF Roborough had proved inadequate and morale worsened across the region with growing fears over the lack of protective fighters and anti-aircraft guns. A number of residents left Falmouth as a result; at Penzance there were concerns that the town had no public or private air-raid shelters and very few gas masks, while the Scilly Islands saw 400 inhabitants leave because of the poor defences against aerial attacks.

On 2 August, German aircraft dropped propaganda leaflets all over the country, with an English translation of Hitler's Reichstag speech declaring his peace terms with Britain and his plans to create a New European Order. Concerned that the leaflets might affect public opinion, British forces hurriedly collected them, annoying the public who were eager to keep them as souvenirs. The following month, however, saw rumours of invasion, with church bells ringing and the Home Guard on alert. German parachutists had landed in Cornwall, everyone was saying; official denials were ignored.

September 1940 would also see the sinking of the *City of Benares*, which had the most profound effect on the mood of people in the south west. The ship was crossing the Atlantic for Canada, carrying evacuees including ninety children, when, on the night of 17 September 1940, it was hit by a German submarine. The children made it to the lifeboats, but it took several hours before they could be rescued – in the rough seas and bitter cold, only thirteen children survived. The tragedy was not reported until a week later, and suddenly there was a change of heart amongst the British population in the south west. Until that moment, despite the attacks on British civilians, there had been public support only for bombing German military targets. As news of the *City of Benares* reached the British, there was a call for reprisals against German civilian targets. In the reports of Mass Observation on 23 September 1940 can be seen the moment the British people went on the attack.

LORD HAW HAW

People in Devon and Cornwall frequently tuned in to Lord Haw Haw, a radio announcer for German propaganda, nicknamed Haw Haw because of his posh English accent. Although the announcements could not, of course, be entirely trusted, he did provide more information than the BBC. Delays by the BBC on reporting the horror of the *Lancastria*'s death toll, for example, made local people wonder what other bad news was being withheld from them.

When the British authorities banned people from listening to Lord Haw Haw, even more people defiantly tuned in. The British public expected to hear the news of France's capitulation 'first from Haw Haw'.

Lord Haw Haw was really William Joyce, an American-born political agitator who had moved to England with his family in 1921 and joined Oswald Mosley's British Union of Fascists (BUF) in 1933. Joyce became director of propaganda, with a reputation as a ferocious orator.

In 1935, Joyce came to Plymouth to try and revive the flagging fortunes of the local BUF branch. He spoke at the Assembly Rooms in Devonport and stayed in the city for a further five weeks. Joyce then set up his own party, the National Socialist League (NSL), which called for Britain to unite with Hitler's Germany against the 'Jewish manifestations' of Bolshevism and international finance.

Just before war was declared, Joyce and his wife fled to Berlin to escape arrest by the British authorities. Once in Berlin, a chance encounter got him an audition on German radio and he replaced Wolf Mittler as the English-speaking propagandist.

The name 'Lord Haw-Haw' was coined by a radio critic of the *Daily Express* newspaper and was designed to satirise Wolf Mittler's exaggerated British accent. There would be many 'Lord Haw Haws', but William Joyce's name became synonymous with German radio propaganda. In Plymouth during the war, there were rumours that Lord Haw Haw lived on a houseboat on Hooe Lake and had been seen in the bar of the lakeside Royal Oak.

In 1941, Mr G.R. Williams was 8 years old in Devonport and remembers his family gathering around their Rediffusion radio set to listen anxiously to Lord Haw Haw's broadcast: 'Germany calling, Germany calling.' Lord Haw Haw warned them that Devonport was next in line to be bombed, and he was right – the Williams family were bombed out of their home. Mr Williams believes that Lord Haw Haw knew the area because William Joyce had lived in Tiverton before the war. (www.plymouthherald.co.uk/Looking/story-15332060-detail/story.html)

When the war ended, Joyce was captured in the woods near Flensburg while gathering firewood and in a desperate state. He was tried at the Old Bailey and hanged for treason at Wandsworth Prison on 3 January 1946.

Lord Haw Haw's propaganda days were over. He hadn't always been right anyway. During the war, he'd announced 'The Germans have sunk HMS *Cicala*', strange when HMS *Cicala* was the navy's name for the Royal Dart Hotel at Kingswear, base of operations for all the coastal forces around Dartmouth. And it's still there – definitely not sunk yet.

CIVIL DEFENCE

On 14 May 1940 the Secretary of State for War asked for all British men between 15 and 65 to offer their services to defend their country: to join an organisation that would be called the Local Defence Volunteers (LDV). In July 1940 Churchill renamed them the Home Guard.

Civil Defence workers file past Lord and Lady Astor at Mount Wise. (THP)

The government hoped to raise a force of 150,000 but in the first few days 400,000 enlisted. In Tavistock, 135 enlisted, including a 79-year-old Boer War veteran. Officially women were not allowed to join until 1943, but unofficially women were active within the Home Guard from the outset and there was even a national association of women called the Amazons, training women to fight.

Within the first six weeks, more than 1 million men had joined the LDV. However, the early LDV forces were heavily criticised for lack of equipment and the poor men would soon to be nicknamed 'Look, Duck and Vanish'. The Cornish LDV were regarded as no more 'effective than pea shooters' partly owing to shortage of rifles.

Why were we so unprepared? In 1938 Prime Minister Neville Chamberlain knew that war was coming even as he famously attempted to make peace with Hitler, waving that embarrassing peace agreement in the air declaring 'Peace in our time!' while Hitler prepared to invade Eastern Europe. In fact Chamberlain's peace-making was an intelligent strategy to give us more time to prepare for war.

In 1938, Britain was not ready. We were gearing up for war on all levels, with factories producing aircraft and tanks, and an intelligence network spreading out across Europe and monitoring all Nazi spies in Britain. We knew the Nazis' war machine could annihilate us. But we just weren't ready. So Chamberlain made an agreement that would give us more time: Hitler concentrated on invading Eastern Europe first, believing that the British would do nothing, at least for a while.

Chamberlain noted 'until our armaments are completed, we must adjust our foreign policy to our circumstances, and even bear with patience and good humour actions which we should like to treat in a very different fashion'. Chamberlain described his strategy to his foreign secretary as:'to hope for the best while preparing for the worst.'

However, when we did declare war, we still weren't ready for it. On 3 September 1939, we had less than 300 aircraft to patrol the entire British coastline; Germany destroyed our intelligence net-work within weeks; and our factories couldn't produce weapons fast enough. (This would improve. By 1942, we were producing aircraft, tanks and munitions faster than the Nazis.) Dunkirk and Operation Aerial left much of our munitions behind in France, often destroyed to keep it out of German hands.

As France fell to the Germans, the southern coast of Britain became the longest siege line in history. And again Britain wasn't ready. So what happened? In June 1940, we changed our strategy. It was the biggest change in military strategy in British history.

It began with a very secret army.

EDMUNDSON
AND FRIENDS

Stuart Edmundson was a Quaker who, prior to the war, ran a ferti-
liser manufacturing business in Plymouth. In 1937 he joined a Devon
Royal Engineer territorial unit and, in July 1940, he was ordered
to report to a Colonel Colin Gubbins in London. Although lots of
Quakers were conscientious objectors during wartime, many also
felt that it was their duty to protect others, such as Jews, from persecution. The Quakers of Plymouth were historically renowned for
being fighters against oppression and perhaps this explains Stuart's
religious justification for joining in the war effort.

Before Dunkirk, Edmundson had established quite an operation
making Molotov cocktails – home-made petrol bombs – at Fort
Austin, a disused Napoleonic fort in Plymouth, for distribution to
the newly formed Local Defence Volunteers. Soon he was touring
Devon and Cornwall instructing the LDV (later renamed the Home
Guard) in the manufacture and deployment of home-made bombs.

Detachment of the Plymouth Home Guard. (THP)

Suddenly Edmundson was ordered to London to meet Colonel Gubbins. Was he in trouble?

Far from it. Stuart Edmundson was exactly the sort of man Gubbins was looking for to train and run a clandestine army in the south west that would 'stay behind' in the event of German invasion and, through terrorist tactics and sabotage, delay any German advance beyond the coastlines. An army so secret Edmundson wasn't even supposed to tell his wife.

Colin Gubbins himself was not the sort of man you'd expect in the British military in 1940 – a guerrilla warrior. In the First World War, he'd witnessed the successes of Russian guerrillas in action. In Ireland, he'd learned a lot about the IRA. He wrote training manuals for Military Intelligence (Research) on guerrilla warfare and the use of explosives and, just before the start of the Second World War, he'd been sent by Military Intelligence (Research) into Europe to consider ways of organising anti-Nazi resistance, ending up in Poland organising guerrilla fighters just as the Germans invaded. He travelled with the exiled Poles to France to continue the work, but the British authorities decided to try his tactics in Norway as Germany advanced. With five Territorial Army units on board fishing trawlers, Gubbins made very successful hit-and-run attacks on the German communication lines, but the Norwegian campaign ultimately turned into a disaster and his troops were withdrawn.

In the meantime, the British Government realised it needed its own resistance organisation in place in the event of a German invasion. Dunkirk and Operation Aerial made the matter even more urgent and, after some false starts, Gubbins was asked to set up the underground secret army, choosing an appropriately vague name: 'Auxiliary Units'.

To call them a secret army is a slight misnomer. Gubbins' studies showed that the most effective guerrilla warriors worked in small groups independently of each other, appearing behind enemy lines as if from nowhere and attacking on their own initiative before completely disappearing again. Therefore, Gubbins established a very loose organisation with intelligence officers in each region to set up the patrols and organise training, but once the Germans invaded, each patrol was effectively on its own. Each built their own secret underground operational bases (OBs), heavily camouflaged, and containing their own supplies of food and munitions.

If the Germans invaded, these men would leave their homes and their families and disappear into the countryside, ready to make furtive attacks on railway lines, docks and communications – destroying and disrupting the infrastructure to make things as difficult as possible for the Germans. Their greatest strengths were their camouflaged locations and their independent initiatives – the British Resistance would not fail while there was a single patrol still operating against the Germans. There was an unspoken agreement that this was a suicide mission.

Gubbins was looking for people with courage and initiative, and Stuart Edmundson, with his Molotov cocktails, was an ideal candidate. He was appointed as intelligence officer for Devon and Cornwall and was soon organising local resistance cells. At the outset, each cell or patrol consisted of a leader and two members so Gubbins was continuously looking for recruits from the Home Guard, with the approval of the commander-in-chief of the Home Forces, Field Marshall 'Tiny' Ironside. The best men for the job were those who had previously worked closely with the landscape and had the survival skills necessary for the task, i.e. gamekeepers, woodsmen or men who were active hikers or mountaineers.

Looking at the appointments across Devon and Cornwall, Edmundson was much broader in his recruitment. His volunteers were also appointed from the local Home Guard groups but were often men of suitable age to join the military yet prevented by their reserved occupations – teachers, blacksmiths, farmers, etc. Land management, health and intelligence were all key attributes of Edmundson's recruits. Some of the underground bases were dug in fields or near land belonging to members of the Auxiliary Patrols. Bases such as these were major undertakings, requiring engineering knowledge to dig out vantage points, space for supplies, and sometimes even plumbing for running water. A number still exist, though often on private land and so inaccessible to the public, but organisations like CART (www.coleshillhouse.com), Cyberheritage (www.cyber-heritage.co.uk) and Hidden Heritage (www.hiddenheritage.org) are actively mapping these sites with some wonderful photographs.

Patrols were generally located on the outskirts of the bigger towns of Devon and Cornwall. Around Plymouth were the Plymstock, Plympton, Tamerton Foliot and Yelverton patrols, with another cluster to the east around Wembury and Ivybridge. If the Germans were to invade Plymouth, these groups would strike from hidden bases around the city's perimeter.

Gubbins intended that his units would, in the event of an invasion, disappear into their bunkers to prepare their attacks. Edmundson, however, modified this in the early months, believing that the sudden disappearance of these men would arouse suspicion. Instead, they were to 'wait it out' – stay in their jobs, behave normally, and then at night secretly strike back.

By 1943, there would be at least thirty-six patrols in Devon and over forty patrols in Cornwall. In time, Edmundson handed the organisation of Cornish defences over to John Dingley, a local banker who lived at Stoke Climsland on the Cornish side of the Tamar River. At first the patrols were not given uniforms, but eventually it was felt that the Home Guard uniform would afford them some protection from being shot on sight. The uniform also gave their training activities some credibility in the eyes of local constables seeking out suspected saboteurs.

Each patrol was issued with a cardboard box of incendiaries and sabotage equipment, following training. Until the bunkers were waterproof, many of these boxes had to be kept in homes, ammunition often stored behind sofas or in the loft.

Stuart Edmundson wasn't supposed to tell his wife about his secret mission, but the 'cases of frightfulness' that turned up at his house in Yelverton quickly made that impossible: grenades, weapons, detonators, all had to be frantically stored away, often with the help of the neighbours.

Fortunately Edmundson would soon establish his stores at Fort Austin, though it might have been a good idea to inform the local army command, VIII Corps. The corps commander heard mysterious explosions coming from Fort Austin after dark and strange rumours that something sinister was going on, so he stationed armed infantrymen around the old Napoleonic fort, determined to catch anyone causing mischief with explosives.

When General Frederick Morgan took over command of VIII Corps, Edmundson felt confident enough to inform the general of the local patrols and the stores at Fort Austin. The general was impressed and offered intelligence information on suitable target sites.

If the Germans invaded, it was agreed that the regular armed forces in Cornwall and Devon would retreat to a new line of defences that ran between Bridgewater and Axminster. The 'stay behinds' would then do their best to destroy the Tamar railway bridge, the Devonport Docks and the fuel supply dumps above Falmouth and outside Torquay. Edmundson agreed with the general's plans though the fuel dumps above Falmouth were a controversial target as Edmundson was worried that the burning fuel would gush into Falmouth and do more damage to the town than the Germans could.

Fortunately the German invasion was postponed indefinitely. The men of the Auxiliary Units would stay prepared throughout the war – prepared to leave their families and homes, prepared to kill with their bare hands if necessary, prepared to destroy and disrupt their own towns and communities. Many kept the secret of their mission for the rest of their lives. Later in the war, some joined the military or the Special Operations Executive (SOE) and took part in active service, their training ideal for the kind of guerrilla warfare needed against the Germans occupying Europe.

In 1944 Captain Stuart Edmundson joined the SOE in Asia, called Force 136, landing in New Delhi on 10 December. Fighting the Japanese was a very different scenario, with European agents unable to disguise themselves and hide amongst the native populations, who were sometimes antagonistic to these foreign 'colonialists'. Force 136's agents had to hide out in the jungle, risking tropical diseases, with only the local Communist resistance fighters willing to help in the attacks on the Japanese.

In August 1945, Edmundson worked for Admiral Lord Louis Mountbatten, Supreme Allied Commander South East Asia (SACSEA), tasked with accepting the surrender of Japanese forces and maintaining public order until the restoration of civil government. A key mission was assisting prisoners of war and their return home. On 30 August 1997, Colonel Stuart Edmundson officially opened the Parham Airfield Museum (www.parhamairfieldmuseum.co.uk).

After the war, the secret stores of explosives and equipment were supposed to be collected, but some were so well hidden they were forgotten. In 1966, a Tavistock labourer drove a pick into a box of squelchy explosives that someone had secretly buried under a tree and two Devonshire old ladies turned up at the local police station with a box of Stuart Edmundson's sabotage equipment. 'Excuse me, officer, we thought you might like this back …'

SPECIAL DUTIES

While the men were secretly training for their guerrilla attacks, a separate organisation was established to spy on any German invaders.

In every region, special duties intelligence officers were recruiting civilian men and women – doctors, midwives, farmers, publicans – as 'cut-outs' who could travel inconspicuously passing secret messages to and from agreed locations, and spies who would operate radio sets in secret (often underground) locations, informing the headquarters of Home Forces on the activities of the enemy invaders.

The spies knew that they would have to remain in their underground bunkers broadcasting until the Germans discovered them – it was yet another suicide mission, though many bunkers had clever escape tunnels to give the radio operator a hope of fleeing. In preparation secret aerials were fixed to trees, bunker entrances hidden under haystacks and outside toilets, and radio sets concealed in attics. There are known to have been nine of these Special Duties substations in Devon and another nine in Somerset (www.coleshillhouse.com/specialdutiesbranch/sds-bunker-locations. php). These homeland agents were encouraged to hide their activities from the local military as well as their friends and families. However, despite their secrecy, their practise signals were sometimes intercepted by local forces searching for German spies.

For security, the Special Duties agents were unknown to the Auxiliary patrols and these spies and 'cut-outs' had no knowledge of the chain of command or the Auxiliary patrol members either. When the Auxiliary Units were asked to train with the regular army, however, these Special Duties spies would often be there, in hiding, secretly practising their espionage techniques. During these manoeuvres, the women of Special Duties would frequently spend five days or more cooped up in their underground bases – called 'zero stations' – practising their radio signals, often strange combinations of letters. The Germans had no idea.

WELLINGTON'S WAR

Margaret and her elder sister Ann grew up in Plympton during the war and remember how their father Cyril taught music and maths at the local school. Margaret was born during an air raid on 3 December 1940 and recalls being evacuated with her mother and sister to Oxfordshire just one day before a bomb hit their neighbour's back garden. They remember their father and his brother Herbert having brilliant singing voices and their father would go on to establish the Plympton Choral Society, often allowing them, as kids, to decorate the stage with flowers for the performances. They knew that Cyril and Uncle Herbert were in the Home Guard. Since both worked in reserved occupations this was their opportunity to 'do their bit for the war effort'.

It wasn't until the daughters discovered their father's meticulously kept diaries, however, that they realised he and Herbert also belonged to an elite squad of 'stay behinds' known as the Plympton Auxiliary Unit Patrol. Margaret and her sister then kindly allowed CART to post an excerpt from the diaries on their website (www. coleshillhouse.com/wartime-diaries-of-captain-cyril-and-doris-wellington.php).

On 5 July 1940, Cyril and his wife Doris witnessed the first German plane dropping bombs on to the city – they thought the bombs fell on Devonport, but perhaps it was attacking the oil tanks at Torpoint. Forty-one bombs fell on their locality in just two weeks and later that month they were busy with their neighbours building an air-raid shelter for both families, under the floor of the Wellingtons' garage.

In June and July 1940, the usual Home Guard training and parades are recorded but, on 28 July, Cyril and Doris mention Cyril going on Special Duty to Elfordleigh – the Plympton Patrol were secretly building their underground Operational Base (OB) though

Family photo of Cyril, Doris, Ann and Margaret Wellington in late 1942 or early 1943. Young Margaret is sat on her mother Doris' lap. (Reproduced with the kind permission of Miss Ann Wellington and Mrs Margaret Gardner)

A photograph of the Plympton Auxiliary Unit Patrol taken at Captain Falcon's house at Cornwood. (Reproduced with the kind permission of CART and Miss Ann Wellington and Mrs Margaret Gardner)

this first attempt was abandoned as unsuitable before the end of 1940 and they built a second base on the edge of Elfordleigh golf course. During the war, Elfordleigh would become a home for evacuated St Barnados kids and the Plympton Patrol would use the grounds (as well as those at Ivybridge, Crownhill and Yelverton) for their training exercises. Boringdon Hall would become a local headquarters for the Home Guard; meetings were often held there and Cyril, in-between training sessions as a 'stay behind', would continue to attend these meetings and perform his Home Guard duties.

His Home Guard uniform arrived on 30 July, soon followed by his HG armlet. In August, his group witnessed the firefights over the Channel, with sixty-six German planes and nineteen 'of ours' shot down on one day alone. At the same time the men were taught to kill silently with fighting knives and Cyril was making bombs and demonstrating the Bren guns – a light machine gun that stood on a bipod stand, usually fired while lying face down on the ground. He spent September 1940 distributing ammunition and rifles to patrol members (the Browning Automatic rifle was preferred over the Winchester 300, it seems). It's likely the patrol also had access to a Thompson machine gun, Enfield rifles, phosphorous grenades and 'sticky bombs'. Explosives and ammunition for these weapons were stored at home, up in the loft, or in the air-raid shelter. Margaret's cousin, Joy (Herbert's daughter), remembers waking up one night and coming out of her bedroom to see her father secretly drying ammunition by the fire.

In the midst of the September bombings, the exhausted patrol were on high alert – British Intelligence told them Hitler's invasion was imminent. The following month the training for the Auxiliary Units took up all their spare time and when, in November, Cyril visited the Holbeton Patrol, there was still talk of Hitler invading any day.

Throughout 1940 and 1941, the air-raid sirens were relentless – often twice a day and four times on 9 November 1940. The family tried to maintain a normal life but the constant anxiety and the scarcity of foodstuffs such as eggs made it difficult. On 16 December, the health visitor brought them a baby gas mask for the new arrival (Margaret) and that Christmas Eve the brothers sang for the troops.

The attack on Plymouth, on 13 January 1941, dropped 10,000 incendiaries, leaving them without gas or electricity for weeks in the middle of winter. Cyril was now spending more time on Auxiliary Unit duties and, from 24 January, Cyril and Herbert spent three days at Coleshill for their first major training session. The weather was appalling and it took over five hours for them to get back home. Another training session, giving instruction in first aid, took place in February and then Captain Edmundson, intelligence officer for the region, inspected the OB at Elfordleigh.

Soon training was offered to become a patrol leader and so Cyril and Herbert tossed a coin to see who would go. Cyril won. Even without the extra training, the spring of 1941 would be both busy and dangerous, with German planes frequently threatening the localities. Easter Sunday would see Cyril taking his daughter Ann to Saltram to see the Allied Wellington bomber that had crashed there returning from a raid on Brest, but soon the raiders of the south west were themselves under attack again. The infamous bombings of April 1941 had started. Incendiaries gutted Cyril's school, leaving only the hall and one classroom, and at Torpoint the oil tanks were set ablaze.

On Sunday, 4 January 1942, the County Final Patrol Competition took place at Okehampton. William Falcon was group leader overseeing Group 2 (comprising Plymstock, Holbeton, Tamerton Foliot and Yelverton patrols) and, although Plympton Patrol lost, he brought them a pheasant as a consolation prize. Cyril would later be promoted to captain in charge of Group 2 and then Herbert would have his turn as Plympton's Patrol leader, a position he still held when Plympton finally won the Patrol Competition in September 1942.

View of the destruction of Plymouth: a photograph taken from the Guildhall Tower. (THP)

On 8 January, Cyril unexpectedly received call-up papers to join the Royal Army Ordinance Corps, responsible for military vehicles and weapons, uniforms and ammunition. They didn't know of his secret mission and wanted him making lists instead. Cyril made an urgent call to the group leader, Captain Falcon, and headed to the call-up in Lincoln to try to explain. Doris was heartbroken, preparing Cyril's kit for the long cold journey to Lincoln, but two days later she was delighted to receive word that he would be coming home – he (and probably his group captain) had successfully convinced the army that Cyril's work in Plympton was more than just Home Guard parades; it was vital to the war effort. The poor man arrived home at 3 a.m. on Sunday, 18 January, having walked all the way from Laira in the pouring rain.

At a time when many historians believe that Britain thought Hitler wouldn't invade after all, the Auxiliary Units were actually still gearing up for invasion. Indeed, the year 1942 saw a significant increase in Cyril Wellington's activity – he was now group captain and visited all the patrols in his area. Night exercises become more frequent and the OB was constantly maintained and inspected. There were mock invasion exercises at Yelverton – 'blacking up' at home in preparation proved to be very funny – and they took part in a large-scale exercise – a mock invasion of Plymouth called Operation Drake that lasted two days. In late March 1942, there was even a mock attack on Dingley's house at Stoke Climsland, though it's not clear whether Dingley was expecting it!

It was a strange war for these men, on constant alert, constantly training, digging and maintaining bases and equipment that ulti-mately weren't used. If the Germans had invaded, they were ready to destroy the railway lines around Plymouth – certainly at Plympton and probably Laira if they could get there. Whether they had enough explosives to destroy the bridges is debatable, but the Devonport Docks would also have been a vital target to disrupt the German Forces. These secret guerrillas were prepared to risk their lives for their country and remained ready to face this ever-present threat – a threat that was all too real – for much of the war.

Special thanks goes to Miss Ann Wellington and Mrs Margaret Gardner for permission to use research from their parents' diary for this book, and to Nina Hannaford from CART for allowing me access to the research and photographs on the CART website, and for putting me in contact with Mrs Gardner.

For more information about the Plympton Patrol and the hundreds of other patrols around Britain, please see CART's excellent website: www.coleshillhouse.com. The Wellingtons' fascinating diary is reproduced on there, along with a full list of all the members of the patrol.

LEBENSRAUM

In early 1939, German spies headed into Britain to prepare for the invasion across the Channel. Merchant ships, the easiest route for these spy missions, were captained by *Dampfer Kapitaen* (the literal translation is 'steamboat captains') who belonged to a special branch of German Naval Intelligence and were known as the DK group. Their speciality was infiltrating foreign ports and military installations. Even before the war, a DK ship had successfully tricked its way into Portsmouth Naval Base to monitor the Royal Navy's wireless communications.

The DK group sent two navy (*Kreigsmarine*) captains, Hans Kirschenlohr and Erwin Schmidt, into the south-west ports disguised as businessmen. Their task: to gather intelligence about every port from Land's End to Margate. Their excellent maps still exist in the Cornwall Record Office: forty maps with photographs of every harbour, illustrations of the topography, notes on any troublesome tides or winds, and profiles of the coastline, indicating landmarks visible from the sea. Here was the list of targets vital for the success of the German invasion. By the time war was declared on 3 September 1939, the commander of the German Navy knew more about the south-west coast of England than the Admiralty in London.

At the same time, Germany's intelligence agency, the Abwehr, had an espionage network in the British Isles comprising 256 men and women. Since 1937 they had been infiltrating British society with deep undercover agents, organised into two networks: the 'R-chain' were mobile agents posing as sightseers and commercial salesmen, travelling around and in and out of the country on 'legitimate business'; the 'S-chain' were sleeper agents from many countries, including Britain, living as normal citizens, blending into everyday life. There were at least ten women in the 'S-chain', two of them in their 50s and working as maids for British admirals. In September 1939, German Intelligence knew the location of every major airfield, munitions factory and military base, though of course their information did not foresee the sudden expansion from 1940 of airbases in England's south west.

Scotland Yard and MI5 did, however, know about the agents. In fact the day Britain declared war on Germany was also probably history's largest round-up of spies – in ten days (visiting homes and places of work) British Intelligence caught 356 people on their 'Class A espionage list'. Hundreds were deported or detained.

Hitler's plans for the invasion of Britain, '*Studie Nordwest*', were finalised in December 1939, and in July 1940 he issued 'Directive 16 for the Preparations of a Landing Operation against England'. The first objective was to destroy the naval ports along England's southern coast, but the Battle of Britain would annihilate such plans.

In September 1940, three German agents managed to secretly enter Plymouth on a French cutter called *La Part Bleu*. Perhaps their mission was to sabotage the docks, although there doesn't seem to be any record of this. They did, however, produce a very detailed map showing the location of the 48th Division in Devon and indicating gaps in the new fortifications around the southern coastline. The map was soon presented to Hitler.

Meanwhile, Germany's invasion of Britain was planned for 3 September 1940. Barges were assembled in Belgian and French ports for German personnel and equipment to be transported across the Channel. And after five days of aerial attacks, Göring believed his Luftwaffe had decimated the RAF. Overconfident, Göring ordered the German planes to attack the London dockyards instead of RAF targets, with horrific casualties. This, however, gave the RAF airfields across southern England a little time to recover, so when the Luftwaffe delivered its 'decisive blow' on 15 September 1940, it was in for a shock. The Battle of Britain was a triumph for the Allied Forces. Just two days later, a secret German signal was intercepted – the invasion of Britain had been postponed.

Refusing to accept failure, the Luftwaffe changed its tactics: bring the British to their knees. On 27 November 1940, 112 German aircraft bombed Plymouth, dropping 100 tons of high explosives. Their targets included RAF Mountbatten in Plymouth Sound and its seaplanes and the oil tanks at nearby Radford – these were considered well camouflaged but a German aerial reconnaissance photograph very clearly reveals the Radford supply base. With intelligence coming from the German spies just months before, the German bombers knew their targets well.

ON THE WATCH LIST

As refugees arrived from Europe, the Exeter Branch of the British Union of Fascists (BUF) advertised for any pro-Nazi sympathisers to join them. Fascist evacuees willing to help the BUF were politely asked to call into their South Street headquarters on Friday or Saturday evenings; a peculiar request considering the suffering of so many of the refugees as the Nazis invaded. Did anyone drop in?

A number of Nazi sympathisers remained on MI5's watch list including Edward D'Alessio, a graduate of the Royal Naval Engineering College at Devonport and leader of Plymouth's branch of Mosley's BUF. Born in India and then educated at Budleigh Salterton, young D'Alessio became a cadet at the Royal Naval College, Dartmouth. In 1927 he left the navy because he suffered from seasickness, though more likely forced out because of his political affiliations.

A bit of a misfit who failed to live up to his own expectations, D'Alessio spent the next ten years travelling and took a series of jobs as a mechanic before returning to the Plymouth BUF eager to show his support for Hitler. He was eventually detained (along with many others) under D Regulation 18B and spend the war in an internment camp. The BUF leader, Sir Oswald Mosley, would be sent to Holloway prison in May 1941.

In January 1940, two other members of the BUF were arrested on suspicion of aiding the enemy. Claude Duvivier had worked at Sanctuary Farm in Woodbury near Exeter. He was Belgian-born, naturalised British, and a fascist since 1936. William Crowle was a welder at Devonport Dockyard, although he was discharged when war broke out because of his BUF membership. He first joined the BUF in 1933 but resigned and then rejoined in 1939, writing to Duvivier about ship movements and complaining about the

British 'cover-up' of casualty figures. They were both sentenced to six months in prison with hard labour and on their release they were interned until after D-Day. At their trial, the judge commented: 'every man was entitled to his own political views but no man had the right to use those views against this country when at war.'

Throughout the war, the Duke of Cornwall Hotel in Plymouth survived the bombing although buildings around it were flattened. The hotel was run by the Welsh family, who were on MI5's watch list from August 1939. Joseph Welsh, the head of the family, was born Joseph Wellisch in Hungary. Before the war, he'd managed the Haymarket Hotel in London and, as a friend of Ribbentrop, Germany's Foreign Minister, Welsh frequently entertained German diplomats at the Haymarket.

In August 1939, he took over the Duke of Cornwall Hotel and, by October 1940, he was on the Suspects List for his pro-German views. His wife was born in England, but of German parentage and educated in Germany. She spoke bitterly of the Jews in Austria and held many strange anti-British theories – apparently it was the British who bombed Pearl Harbour to bring the Americans into the war.

Many American soldiers frequented the Duke of Cornwall Hotel's dances where Welsh's daughter-in-law Bebe happily danced with them, taking officers to her bedroom each night. In October 1943 she was pregnant but still suspiciously intimate with one member of the US Forces. Local authorities believed that she was not a prostitute, but was extracting information from this string of lovers, though they could not prove this information ever reached the enemy. Bebe's brother Emmerich was a member of the British Union of Fascists and Bebe declared that she'd been on a minesweeper and an American submarine, but still there was no proof of her intentions …

Bebe's husband, Henry Welsh, was spotted suspiciously taking photographs of a searchlight battery in August 1939 and later at a tribunal declared himself a conscientious objector. But not to his wife's behaviour, it seems!

In Spring 1944, before the Allied invasion, the Welsh family were forced to leave the south west. Strange that the Duke of Cornwall Hotel was never bombed …

MOREAU
IN TROUBLE

While England was preparing to 'fight them on the beaches', Hubert Moreau was trapped on a beach in France. Landing in the pale moonlight, waves breaking on the shore, the air suddenly filled with angry shouts in German accents and a flurry of torchlight. Moreau and his assistant Le Corre dived for cover behind partly submerged rocks, water up to their necks. They had definitely landed on the wrong beach.

Le Petit Marcel, Moreau and crew had arrived at Le-Guilvinec from Falmouth on 27 July 1940. Earlier in the evening they'd been spotted off the coast by a German aircraft that had dropped a flare warning them they were outside the authorised 4-mile fishing zone. With the boat now anchored in the darkness 300 metres off shore, Moreau and le Corre had landed in a dinghy, only to dive back into the water – the Germans were chasing someone. Could the Germans have spotted them?

Clutching the rocky shore as they floundered in the sea, they found themselves face to face with a breathless fugitive also hiding behind the rocks. Moreau considered offering to help the man and take him back with them to England, but was worried about endangering the mission. With a heavy heart, he beckoned Le Corre and they swam around the frightened man and found another route off the beach.

Dripping wet, they cautiously made their way through the village. Heavy footfalls sent them scurrying into a corner, but the German soldier walked on past them. Their destination was Le Corre's parents' house – it seemed a good idea at the time but

Le Corre's terrified parents explained to them that they couldn't have chosen a worse location and that a villa on the nearby shore had been commandeered by the Germans as the local headquarters. The manhunt they'd witnessed had been a fight between German soldiers, the fugitive a German. Moreau breathed a sigh of relief that he hadn't offered the enemy fugitive a trip back to England.

But now they'd put everyone in the village in danger. If the Germans spotted Moreau or Le Corre acting suspiciously, innocent villagers were likely to be shot in retaliation. And then Moreau realised that he'd made a terrible mistake – as morning came, the Germans would spot their dinghy still on the beach, a small metal plate fixed to it announcing 'Made in Cornwall'. Nothing for it: he would have to go back and hide the dinghy.

He changed clothes into something more like those of a local fisherman – the wooden-soled sabots being rather appropriate for an agent saboteur, though they hurt like hell. Leaving Le Corre with his parents, Moreau strolled casually along the beach to take the dinghy back to *Le Petit Marcel*. Fortunately it was already 4.30 a.m. and other fishermen were about, so Moreau didn't look too suspicious to the German sentry as he rowed away from the beach in the dinghy.

Back on board *Le Petit Marcel*, Moreau's other crewmen, Le Goff, Baltas and Guénolé, were relieved to see him, later than expected but safe. They set off for nearby Beg-Meil, where Moreau hoped to meet his friends, the Gauchards, who'd helped him escape the first time. Moreau had arranged to meet Le Corre at the Gauchards' house at 10 p.m. that night.

On the water they met with French fishermen who immediately spotted they weren't local and kindly offered some disturbing advice: *Le Petit Marcel* stuck out like a sore thumb. It was a motor pinnace for a start, not even rigged for sail, when no one in France had petrol any more. In addition to the 300 litres of petrol in the tank, Moreau and company had many 40-gallon barrels of petrol on the deck, conspicuous from quite a distance. A little humiliated, Moreau took notes for future voyages.

Arriving at Beg-Meil was another mistake; the beach was swarming with sunbathing German soldiers. But Moreau was willing to attempt a landing again in the dinghy and wandered up the beach, trying to look natural with his oars casually over his shoulder, making his way precariously between half-naked Germans.

Suddenly a group of German soldiers called him over. They were trying to repair their motorboat on the beach and, in a mix of mime and bad French, they asked Moreau if he had an adjustable spanner. Moreau thought it best to be friendly and made his way all the way back to *Le Petit Marcel* to fetch the Germans a spanner. It seemed a good idea at the time …

When he eventually made it to his friends' house, Madame Gauchard was delighted to see him, but unfortunately her husband was away and had taken the car. Meanwhile, Le Corre wasn't going to make it to Beg-Meil unless he got a lift from the Germans. No cars, no ferries running, no petrol, no transport – normal life in France had vanished within days of the Germans' arrival. Moreau's plans weren't going well.

It was too dangerous to stay any longer, so Moreau walked back down the beach towards the dinghy. Again the Germans called him over. What now? Smiling, they returned Moreau's spanner.

Back on the *Le Petit Marcel*, Moreau and his crew hurried back to Le-Guilvinec hoping to catch Le Corre before he attempted in vain to travel to Beg-Meil. Alongside the other returning fishing boats, they moored the motor pinnace in the mouth of the estuary, near the breakwater, ready for a quick getaway.

At Le Corre's parents' house it was bad news – Le Corre had set out for Beg-Meil that morning. Moreau left a message that they would try to collect Le Corre on their next visit, praying he hadn't already been captured by the Germans.

It was now after curfew so Moreau, Baltas and Guénolé slipped back to the dinghy, but on reaching their mooring they discovered *Le Petit Marcel* was nowhere to be seen.

They'd left Le Goff with strict orders not to leave the boat or fall asleep. Had he panicked and taken off back to Falmouth?

Now it has to remembered that, apart from Moreau, these men were civilians, just fishermen, so what had happened is as much Moreau's fault as Le Goff's. Moreau frantically scoured the harbour for another boat they could steal back to England and during the search, in the dim light, was surprised to see what he thought might be *Le Petit Marcel*'s silhouette against the breakwater at the harbour entrance. Well it sort of looked like *Le Petit Marcel*.

The three agents hurried to the breakwater to discover *Le Petit Marcel* was high out of the water, tipped on her side at a 45-degree angle. They could now walk around her without getting their feet wet – so much for a fast getaway – and were literally stuck wait-ing hours for high tide in the hope they could shift her.

But what had happened to Le Goff?

Moreau crawled inside the tilted boat. Everything was in disarray. All their provisions were swimming in spilled red wine and machine oil. There was water in the engine room but there seemed to be no damage to the ship. Moreau cursed Le Goff – where on earth was the errant crewman? – only to find Le Goff in his bunk, unconscious with drink, covered with clutter that had crashed on to him as the ship lurched to the shore. It seemed even that had not roused him from his drunken stupor.

The boat would not float again until 10 a.m. – on a Saturday when many fishermen did not go out. Not only were they up high and dry on the wrong part of the shore, but as the sun rose there would be plenty of bystanders contemplating their predicament. So much for being inconspicuous. What to do?

And so at dawn, Moreau and his crew found themselves looking busy, cleaning the hull of a ship that didn't actually need cleaning and pretending to repair a propeller that most definitely was not broken. Any sailors would know they were in the wrong place for such a job, but Moreau hoped the locals wouldn't give them away.

As they pretended to clean and hammer, the German sentry on the breakwater seemed delighted by the distraction and came over, smiling. The sentry even tried to see if he was strong enough to help them turn the propeller. Fortunately the German failed to notice the drums of petrol on the deck or that the pinnace lacked the name and number that all boats were now required to display. The German couldn't get the propeller to turn either – fortunately Moreau had already secured it fast – so he said something affable and encourag-ing in German and still smiling went on his way.

At 8 a.m., though, the trouble started. A maritime police officer arrived on his bicycle and, recognising Guénolé as a local, started asking questions – where were their papers, their registration plate, what on earth were they doing? A curious crowd gathered.

Moreau quickly intervened, demanding to know if the officer was working for the Germans. The officer looked affronted – a good sign – and replied he worked for the local administrator, Québriac. This was very lucky as Québriac had once worked for Moreau's father. 'Then let's go see the administrator,' Moreau declared.

The crowd went ominously quiet as Moreau was dragged away and up some stairs to the administrator's office. Moreau knew the interrogation would go better without the officer's presence, so the minute they reached the administrator's office door, Moreau walked straight in without knocking, told the officer to wait outside and slammed the door in the surprised officer's face.

It was a good move. Moreau, now alone, turned to the bewildered Administrator Québriac who asked, 'Why are you here?'

'I don't have any papers for that boat over there.'

'Is it your boat?'

'Yes.'

And, even more impatiently at being interrupted with such a petty matter, the administrator asked, 'What is this all about?'

'We've come from England,' Moreau declared. 'We're about to return, but we haven't time to equip ourselves with papers and permits at the Kommandantur.'

Québriac sprang to his feet in astonishment. 'At last!'

Moreau had found an ally. Québriac dismissed the officer waiting at the door and told Moreau to take a seat, offering him a cigarette. The administrator remembered Moreau's admiral father very well and was more than happy to offer any intelligence Moreau needed. Forced to act as a liaison officer with the occupying Germans, Québriac was a valuable source of information and – even better – he gave Moreau a stock of blank forms for crew lists and customs clearance already stamped and signed for use on future voyages to France.

It was nearly high water, so Moreau said farewell to his new contact. Québriac promised to seek out and help Le Corre, and Moreau rejoined his crew, much to their relief. They'd pumped the water out of the engines and, as the tide rose, the ship floated, and the crowd and the smiling German sentry waved them off.

After a last hiccup with a failing engine that needed some repairs, by next morning they were in sight of the English coast. The signal station at Pendennis Castle challenged them and when they failed to reply – not actually sure what they were supposed to reply – the station fired a shot across their bows in true buccaneering fashion. *Le Petit Marcel* was boarded, the crew quickly recognised and allowed to proceed. At Falmouth, they were greeted with relief.

It had been a strange first voyage, not entirely successful, but the information and paperwork, and particularly the French contacts they'd made, would enable their return. Moreau found a new fishing boat – no conspicuous petrol this time – and was soon heading back for more dangerous adventures in France.

PIP JARVIS IN
DANGEROUS WATERS

It was a calm night on Cornwall's Helford River, a good night for testing the new equipment, or so Pip Jarvis thought as he positioned the surfboard on the water. Being careful of the Bren gun secured to the nose, Jarvis lay face down on the 15-foot board and paddled out into the darkness.

Ishmael (Pip) Jarvis of the Inshore Patrol Flotilla. (Reproduced with the kind permission of his son, Philip Jarvis)

In the moonlight, he could just about make out the pale shorelines broken by overhanging trees. At the river mouth there was only dark water and a steady breeze caused the board to rock a little in the swell. His boss, Nigel Warington Smyth, was full of good ideas for improving the beach landings, but perhaps, Jarvis thought, this wasn't one of his better ones.

It was 1943 and the Inshore Patrol Flotilla had been making successful landings on the French beaches for a while now, but getting the agents and equipment from the anchored boat and on to the shore was still proving difficult.

Attempted landings through the rough surf had lost them numerous dinghies, many just disappearing after capsizing, resulting in aborted missions and lost supplies. Jarvis' boss, Lieutenant Commander Nigel Warington Smyth, was determined they could find a better way.

So here was Jarvis in deep water trying out the new surfboard and it wasn't really working for him. Yes, lying on his stomach made for a low silhouette which couldn't easily be spotted by German sentries. And you had to admit it was quiet – too many landings had been heard by the Germans, resulting in agents landing under enemy fire – but manoeuvring the over-long surfboard was difficult. He had to move his whole body left or right and paddle hard to turn. Landing on a French beach on this thing was going to take a lot of practice.

At least the Bren gun on board would give them a chance to shoot back. It was a light machine gun, often fired from just this kind of prone position, but normally he'd be lying still on land. Swaying on the water, Jarvis found that the top-mounted magazine made it almost impossible to see where he was going.

He thought he'd better test the machine gun before making a final turn back to the base. He tried to aim, but the gun's vertical movement was limited. Lining up a target was almost impossible as he had to paddle hard left or right to move the whole surfboard into position, and the swell kept him in constant motion. On a calm night, it was difficult, but in surf, it would be impossible to hit anything. Warington Smyth was not going to be happy with Jarvis' assessment – it was back to the drawing board.

There was no one about so Jarvis fired off a few bursts of tracer along the river.

And all hell broke loose. Suddenly the night was full of air-raid sirens. Were the Germans attacking?

Jarvis frantically looked around him, but there were no signs of enemy aircraft. And then it dawned – the local air-raid warden had seen his tracer fire and thought Helford was under attack.

So much for the secret testing. Warington Smyth was definitely not going to be pleased.

Ishmael Jarvis preferred to be known as Pip. He was born in Newcastle and at 14 became a coal miner. When war was declared, he tried to join the Royal Navy like his older brother Joe, but Pip was too young so he worked with the local Home Guard until he was old enough. His first naval experience was with minesweepers, a dangerous job destroying the German mines dropped into the shipping channels, but for young Pip Jarvis even this was too repetitive – so when an officer called for volunteers for 'hazardous work', Pip jumped at the chance for some excitement and found himself joining the Special Services Unit.

Many of the volunteers for these secret missions came from minesweepers. They seemed to be just the kind of men that the British Secret Intelligence Service (SIS) were looking for – good naval experience, not afraid of danger or the unknown and able to work in teams in tough conditions.

While Moreau was completing his third mission into occupied France, the British were creating their own clandestine fleets. There was an urgent need to get intelligence agents into France, get supplies to the Resistance and a growing demand to rescue downed airmen from the French coast and bring them home. After the fall of France, the British and French Forces had tried to get back into France using Motor Torpedo Boats (MTBs) but these efforts had largely been unsuccessful. The MTBs were just too conspicuous, too easily spotted by the enemy as they approached the coast.

Meanwhile, there was a battle going on between different sections of British Intelligence. While the Intelligence Services' transport

Pip Jarvis in the front (with an unknown sailor) in a two-man canoe on the Helford River. (Reproduced with the kind permission of his son, Philip Jarvis)

Pip Jarvis, second row, second from the left. (Reproduced with the kind permission of his son, Philip Jarvis)

operations under Commander F.A. Slocum were attempting to get agents into France to gather information, Churchill himself had established the Special Operation Executive (SOE) under Colonel Colin Gubbins as head of operations to 'set Europe ablaze'. Gubbins had successfully established Britain's secret resistance army of 'stay behinds' and now Churchill wanted him to sabotage the German occupation of France.

Both sections of the Intelligence Services needed transport to get into occupied France and aircraft were in such demand that the only way across the Channel was by sea. But the two sections were at loggerheads – the subversive (explosive) actions of SOE agents would undoubtedly undermine any clandestine activities by the secret intelligence agents. Their missions had incompatible objectives, yet they desperately needed the same transport.

So the early days of the secret flotillas are a bizarre history of multiple, often conflicting, attempts to get across the same body of water, but there were only so many agents with the required knowledge of the sea and in particular navigating the Channel coastlines. If ever there was a case of too many generals and not enough soldiers … But these soldiers would come in the form of skilled volunteers like Jarvis and in the form of civilian fishermen, those same fishermen who had escaped France by fishing boat in the exodus of 1940.

GERRY HOLDSWORTH

While Hubert Moreau's boss Dunderdale was establishing a small flotilla of fishing boats at Mylor Creek near Falmouth, the British Intelligence Service requisitioned a refugee Belgian motor yacht in Newlyn, Cornwall, and made an attempt to cross the Channel.

Among the Intelligence Service personnel was Captain Gerry Holdsworth, an experienced yachtsman and a lieutenant in the Royal Navy. Just before the war, he'd been a member of the Royal Cruising Club, secretly tasked with familiarising himself with areas of the continental coastline that might prove to have strategic importance. When war broke out, he worked with Colonel Gubbins and Section D, mounting very successful hit-and-run raids in Norway using fishing boats. He then helped Gubbins establish the British resistance. In Newlyn, Holdsworth was again working for Gubbins and the SOE, who were now eager to attack the French coastline with hit and run raids. (In 1945, Holdsworth and Gubbins established the Special Services Club behind Harrods in London, celebrating the lives and missions of members of the SOE. It's still there: http://sfclub.org/index.php?page=about-the-club)

Newlyn, where Gerry Holdsworth worked alongside Colonel Gubbins and the Special Operations Executive. (Library of Congress, LC-DIG-ppmsc-08227)

Holdsworth was a formidable character; a true buccaneer, informal in his dealings with the men but if he was upset he 'was like a tiger'. In 1940, he was irritated by British Intelligence's inability to get back into occupied France. Arriving at Newlyn, he was unimpressed by the motor yacht which was slow and noisy and his misgivings were justified when they quickly came under fire from a German convoy. The mission was aborted.

There were ten subsequent attempts, but each time terrible weather or enemy fire drove their motor yacht back to Newlyn. On 11 October, agents trying to land at Anse-de-Bréhec were machine-gunned and the whole operation was abandoned.

Moreau's motor pinnace had also been too conspicuous among the French sailing boats and Holdsworth knew that the only way they could covertly reach the French coast would be under sail. The Free French were having some successes with fishing vessels, proving Holdsworth's point, and there were rumours that the Polish were successfully using feluccas under sail to rescue stranded Poles from the French beaches. Immediately Holdsworth was assigned the task of establishing a British sailing fleet that could get SOE agents into occupied France.

On 5 November 1940, Holdsworth obtained permission to establish a small base in the Helford River, which flows into the west of Falmouth Bay. Overhung by oak trees, the wide yet secluded river is the age-old haunt of smugglers. Holdsworth and his wife Mary established a headquarters at 'Ridifarne' on the north bank. Appropriately this was the summer retreat of the family who made the Bickford fuse used in Cornish mining – the Bickford fuse would become the essential ingredient in SOE's demolition charges.

Holdsworth was allowed to select a dozen volunteer naval ratings from the Royal Naval Patrol Service at Lowestoft to join his crew. Although on naval pay, it was important they were permitted to wear civilian clothes – in fact, disguise themselves as French fishermen pretending to be at work off the French coast, sailing under French colours. There would be no defensive weapons other than light arms and these would be perilous journeys, not just because of the weather conditions, but officially these men no longer had any status – if caught, the crew were likely to be shot on sight as spies.

Ian Fleming of Naval Intelligence (and later writer of the James Bond novels) sent red-haired John 'Bunny' Newton to join

Holdsworth's crew. Newton was a Guernsey fisherman and notorious smuggler, the sort of man who 'gets things' for you and you don't ask where he got them. Also among the volunteers was a Breton fisherman called Pierre Guillet who had been dragged off his tunny fishing boat by a British warship and interrogated in Plymouth. Fortunately for Holdsworth, Guillet was only too happy to help them disguise their own boats as tunny fishing vessels for the journeys back to France.

Their first transport was a 60-foot French yawl called the *Mutin* (the '*Rebel*'). Though a French Navy training ship, she could cope with heavy seas and could be disguised, with Guillet's help, to resemble a typical tunnyman fishing in the Bay of Biscay. While Holdsworth was having her fitted with a powerful diesel engine, he acquired a very small seaplane tender from the RAF which would be called simply RAF 360.

Both ships needed fitting with wireless transmitters, set with Air Force frequencies so any German interceptions would mistakenly think they were looking for aircraft not boats, but volunteer Len Macey described the problems they had with the radio aerials:

> I'm tacking all these wires along and eventually we get the sets working and then we have a big problem because they've got a bloody big aerial up there and it works beautifully with this, but when Holdsworth comes aboard he said, 'The French will know it's [an aerial] so you can't have it, you've got to do something else'. So we thought of some way of winding the aerial all around the rigging or we made a special rigging for it just to look like rigging and that worked very well.

Training along the English coast in all weathers had its own hazards. Pip Jarvis remembered being out in the fishing boat and having to duck into St Ives Harbour to escape the stormy weather. Suddenly the ropes tying the ship to the quay were coming loose and an officer shouted 'Abandon ship!'. But that was more difficult than it sounded – one second the boat was 10 feet below the quay, the next 10 feet above. When to jump became a matter of life or death, as landing in the water could get you killed. Jarvis managed to jump and land on the quayside, but the boat broke her moorings in the storm and was washed away. Next morning, they found the fishing boat washed up in nearby Carbis Bay. They'd had a lucky escape.

Brook Richards, soon to become a member of the crew, first heard about some 'goings-on' between Falmouth and Brittany when he was in hospital in November 1940, recovering from a broken leg after his minesweeping ship sank off Falmouth. Bill Ford, who passed on this information, was an old friend and a retired naval officer. He knew Brittany well (having built a yacht over there), and he said he'd seen a little group of Breton sailing ships in Falmouth but they couldn't be fishing as there was no ice to preserve the fish and no fuel. To Bill and Brook, it was obvious they were there to make contact with occupied France. So Brook Richards sent a note to the British authorities, tongue-in-cheek, suggesting that a good way to get into occupied France would be using Breton fishing boats. It took the authorities a few months but Brook Richards was eventually hauled into an office in London and interviewed – was he in trouble? No – he was offered the job working as second-in-command to Gerry Holdsworth, head of the Helford Flotilla.

Richards' first job, and the first mission for RAF 360, meant navigating a fishing boat to the Brittany coast to meet some unusual members of the Polish intelligence network Interallié – an old Frenchman and his son who evaded the German patrols by rowing about 6 miles downriver to the coast to meet them. To make the meet, RAF 360 arrived as the moon rose, dangerously increasing the chances of the Germans spotting them.

Pierre Guillet sat up forward on the deck, scanning the horizon for the agreed landmark – the lighthouse on the Île-de-Batz. If they missed this, they wouldn't make it in time to meet their contacts. From there the RAF 360 made its slow approach across the tide to Le-Trépied. The jagged Brittany shoreline is treacherous and tides 13-metres high rip at terrifying speeds. Fortunately, Guillet knew every inch of that coastline and the knowledge of the volunteering Breton fishermen became invaluable, particularly on dark nights.

As the single-masted boat appeared, Richards spotted the old bearded man and his son. The RAF 360 approached cautiously, keeping the submachine guns trained on the visitors – it might still be a trap. Even when the expected parcel was handed across, Holdsworth quickly took it below to check if it was a bomb. But the mission was a success and the precious parcel safely arrived back at Helford – despite an elderly British customs officer demanding Holdsworth open it for inspection. Crewman Len Macey, who was on board the RAF 360 during this expedition, described the mission:

The dangers were part of the excitement. Directly we got over there, there was a feeling of tension that went all through the boat. Everything was so quiet and when people spoke it was only to relay an order that was to be carried out. Then you heard them coming and you took them aboard and just got out of it … I think on a small boat you get used to being out there in the elements. You see things that other people perhaps don't see. When you are looking for something and then suddenly it appears there's always great excitement. I remember one pretty rough night we met this chap in a boat. He was sculling in the French way, with one hand, and he'd got this little boy with him who he was telling what to do as they came alongside. I think he was very pleased that we had been able to find him in such rough weather. He gave us a parcel which we brought back to London … I never knew what was in it.

Agents of the Special Operations Executive rarely if ever knew what the packages were or who they were transporting. Sometimes they didn't even know they were actually working for the SOE.

On his first trip on the *Mutin*, Macey picked up six or seven men wearing suits, overcoats and Homburg hats, all sitting there in a rubber dinghy in the middle of the ocean waiting to be collected. Macey declared, 'I realised we were doing something extraordinary, but I didn't know anything about it, like who they were or where they were going.'

Lieutenant Brook Richards, conscious of the danger of their situation, was concerned about protecting the *Mutin* from machine-gun fire. Concrete bolted on to the wheelhouse wasn't going to help them look like a fishing boat, and magnetic armour would affect their compass readings, so it had to be non-magnetic armour. This non-magnetic armour was too expensive at £600 but a few bottles of whisky to the petty officer at Falmouth's navy dockyards got them some and just in time …

Just 20 miles from the Scillies the crew on the *Mutin* were expecting to rendezvous with a British Beaufighter aircraft. At the right time, an aircraft duly appeared and the *Mutin* flashed its recognition signal, only to be strafed from end to end by the plane's 20-millimetre cannon. They'd been spotted by a German Focke-Wulf aircraft, very like a Beaufighter when seen head-on. The German plane quickly came around and hit them with another dose.

Gerry Holdsworth and Brook Richards managed to shelter behind the armour round the wheelhouse, but one of their crewman, still out on deck, was shot. John Newton, the Guernsey smuggler, proved his worth and tended to the dying man as they raced to the

Scillies, all the while with the sea crashing over the deck on top of them. Sadly the crewman died before they made it home.

Tom Long joined the team after the first few missions. He'd been working on a destroyer when he was chosen for Special Service though he didn't know what Special Service meant until he arrived at Helford. At first it seemed an idyllic location, but as he rowed past the *Mutin* the job looked a little more dangerous than he had thought: 'there were shipwrights digging out shrapnel from all over the vessel and patching it up and there was a heap of sails there, they had blood and they were all shot up, and I thought, Jesus Christ, what the hell have I let myself in for now?'

Landings on the beaches were extremely high-risk operations, as Tom Long discovered steering the *Mutin* on moonless nights directed only by Pierre Guillet's knowledge of the coast. Even getting to the shore to drop and hide supplies for the French Resistance (what Holdsworth would call 'Lardering') was hazardous, with rubber dinghies often capsizing in the surf. Tom Long remembers the 'Helford containers' for the Resistance, packed full of incendiary devices. One remarkable invention was the 'exploding rats' – the idea was that someone might find a mangy rat in their factory and shovel it into the furnace, where the rat (packed with explosives) would ignite and shut down the factory.

Signalling between the beach and the offshore ship also demanded ingenuity, so the British invented a kind of luminous golf ball. This was difficult for the Germans to spot but, when held up, it could be seen easily by the waiting ship. Here was age-old smuggling with a twentieth-century twist.

As the days lengthened into the spring of 1941, night landings became more difficult so the *Mutin* took her place in the genuine French fishing fleet in the Bay of Biscay. Making friends with the locals, the *Mutin* delivered huge quantities of explosives cunningly disguised as fish, to be taken far inland, ready for the start of the Allied invasion. Of course, no one was to know that the Allied invasion wouldn't happen for another three years, by which time the fish would surely be starting to smell.

JACQUES GUÉGUEN

Meanwhile the old man and his son from the boat near Le-Trépied were in trouble. They were 71-year-old Jacques Guéguen and his

16-year-old son François, and, on 31 January 1941, they were arrested by the Germans. This was terrible news as Jacques hadn't just been an agent of the Interallié intelligence network; in his 8.4-metre half-decked sloop he had made at least four voyages to British soil in 1940, helping people escape. The Germans, quite rightly, were suspicious of his activities.

As Jacques was taken away by the Germans, he was worried that he'd left a comprising packet for the Interallié network in a drawer in his house. Fortunately, another agent's wife, Anne Le Duc, managed to destroy the package before the Germans found it and Jacques and his son were able to declare their innocence until they were eventually released. At around the same time a local 16-year-old French lad had been found in possession of a plan for the German airbase and was executed. The Germans were cracking down on espionage in France.

In early 1942, Jacques was again back in prison, but temporarily released due to his chronic rheumatism. He was summoned to appear at Rennes Prison on 14 February 1942, but asked an old friend and ally Ernest Sibiril to help him and his son François escape to England instead. On 10 February, Sibiril took them to Fowey on board his 7-metre fishing boat the *André*. A Belgian intelligence officer and a senior French nursing sister escaped with them, and this became the start of one of the most successful escape routes of the war. Between February 1942 and February 1944, Ernest Sibiril and his father organised the escape of 193 people from their boatyard to the shores of south-west England, a remarkable story that is rightly now part of Breton folklore.

Hearing of the arrival of the Guéguens, Brook Richards took the RAF 360 east to Fowey and discovered Jacques Guéguen's boat abandoned, lying in moorings half-full of water. The vessel was towed back to Helford, repaired with a new mainsail, and she was regularly used by Tom Long and Pierre Guillet for an evening's fishing after a long day. Guéguen's boat was called the *Pourquoi-Pas?* – a wonderful name for a boat that saved people's lives, but '*Why Not?*' is still a strange name. Was that really the name of the boat? While being questioned at the Royal Patriotic School at Fowey, Jacques Guéguen had been asked the name of his boat. He'd shrugged and said '*Pourquoi-Pas?*' – perhaps it was a jest, perhaps a mistake in translation, but she would always be known as the *Pourquoi-Pas?* at Helford.

THE WARINGTON SMYTHS

During 1942 conflicts continued between Special Operation Executive personnel and the operational head of the British Intelligence Service, Commander F.A. Slocum. In early 1942, Slocum's sea-faring unit became attached to the Naval Intelligence Division, greatly enhancing Slocum's authority and making things even more difficult for the SOE staff at Helford.

Slocum declared that Holdsworth's fishing vessels at Helford did not look enough like the French ships to go unnoticed; a little pedantic perhaps, considering the British Intelligence Service had help from Breton fishermen. Colin Gubbins, now a brigadier and looking the part with his trimmed moustache, hurried down to Helford to negotiate with Holdsworth, offering four new vessels as replacements approved by the Naval Intelligence Division. But, just as they were about to set sail on their first mission, Hitler's forces invaded Vichy France.

It was a major blow. Now the whole of France was occupied by German militia, making beach landings by boat all the more difficult. Slocum immediately placed a ban on all SOE operations to the west of France, for fear of their raids undermining the Secret Intelligence Services' mail service. And anyway, SOE were at last making secret landings in France by Lysander aircraft with the help of the RAF. With all those 'landings by moonlight', did they really need the flotilla at Helford any more?

For Holdsworth, it was the last straw. He'd had enough and, handing control of SOE's Helford base over to Lieutenant Commander Bevil Warington Smyth, he took his *Mutin*, many of his personnel and his SOE operation to the Western Mediterranean in December 1942.

New commander Bevil Warington Smyth had lost a foot flying in the Fleet Air Arm. His father was the resident naval officer in the Helford River, living at Calamansac overlooking the sheltered berth at Port Navas, the only inlet of the Helford that stayed calm when the east wind got up. The remaining Helford team made a few runs to the coast of Brittany, continuing Holdsworth's 'Lardering' operations, but the Germans' stranglehold on the French coastline was making it even more difficult for the French Resistance to collect the much-needed supplies.

Slocum's Motor Torpedo Boats at Dartmouth were having the same problem. Intelligence agents just weren't getting through. It would take time and a major reorganisation of their resources, along with some new inventions by Bevil's brother Nigel Warington Smyth, before they could re-establish sea lines to France.

In June 1943, it was at last realised that all the fleets of fishing boats and motor boats for SOE and the intelligence services would work best together under a central command. Slocum was appointed to a newly created post, as Deputy Director Operations Division (Irregular) – Slocum would often be referred to simply as DDOD (I). The post gave him the authority to call upon naval commands and bases for all clandestine operational needs.

Slocum appointed Bevil's brother, Lieutenant Commander Nigel Warington Smyth, as the senior officer of a new amalgamated flotilla – the Inshore Patrol Flotilla (IPF), encompassing all operations for the Intelligence Services and SOE between Helford and Dartmouth. As the fishing vessels were brought to one location at Helford, the flotilla became quite a fleet: nine Breton fishing vessels and two large trawlers (including Raymond Le Corre's old ship the *Korrigan*, renamed 2027 for operational purposes). Most had been fitted with new engines to make the journey across the Channel that little bit faster.

The main depot ship was *Sunbeam II*, a three-masted schooner which acted as the communications centre for all the IPF's ships at sea; they used a secure wireless transmitter and were connected directly to DDOD(I) by 'scrambler' telephone. While officers stayed at Ridifarne, the other ranks at Helford, including Pip Jarvis, slept aboard *Sunbeam II*.

At last the Admiralty was happy – the sorties across the Channel were no longer an amateur operation, but organised on military lines. However, there was still the problem of landing on surf beaches and even the Admiralty couldn't find a solution for that. Not yet, anyway.

THE MISSION TO ABER BENOÎT

Agent Maho, real name Pierre Hentic, had a problem. It was October 1943 and he was looking for a sea route to transport vital intelligence information from France to Britain. However, since the Germans had invaded Vichy France, there seemed to be no one in Brittany able to help him – the Germans had infiltrated the escape lines through France, killing many of the Resistance who had been furtively escorting downed airmen and escaping prisoners of war across France and back to Britain. Now the remaining Resistance forces were overwhelmed with a backlog of evaders and escapees, hiding for months in barns and attics with nowhere left to go. Something had to be done about this bottleneck or Maho's intelligence operation would fail.

Maho contacted DDOD (I) who agreed to send a gunboat to the Brittany coast to collect Maho's packet of mail, and also bring back at least a dozen of the stranded airmen. DDOD (I) agreed to it; trouble was he had no idea how they were going to achieve it.

First there was a problem of location – the Germans had established blockhouses and sentry points on every headland along the coast, so Maho suggested the Aber Benoît estuary. Yes, the Germans were on every headland there too, but at low tide the evaders could make their way on to the strand stretching out beyond the shoreline, out to the tidal islets of Rosservor or Tariec. It was a nightmare scenario. The wide river at Aber Benoît is a spectacular location by day, but by night the outer estuary and coast is a deathtrap of rip tides, rocks and shallows. The Germans would never expect the Allies to attempt it, and that alone made it their best option.

Speed was essential. They couldn't wait for the vagaries of wind and tide, so a Motor Gun Boat would have to make the journey, but Slocum knew that the MGBs they had were unreliable. He'd been waiting nearly eighteen months for the new and improved 500 series – MGB 501 had arrived on time, only to be sunk by an accidental explosion. There were still no signs of 502 or 503, and the mission code-named ENVIOUS was set for the night of 3 and 4 November 1943 – the team was just going to have to make do with what was available: MGB 318.

MGB 318 set out from Falmouth on time and in good weather, but their luck didn't last long. The swell picked up so they had to reduce their speed; one engine suffered fuel starvation which meant fuel had to be pumped by hand throughout the mission; and then, as they approached the dark shore, a mist rose and both their navigation and echo-sounding equipment failed. To make matters worse, the Ushant Lighthouse was shining brighter than usual, telling them that German boats were expected. It was a terrifying moment. They were sailing blind in enemy territory.

Nevertheless, just after midnight they approached the agreed rendezvous, the islet of Rosservor, and received the correct flashing signals from the mainland confirming their position and the pickup. The dinghies went out, but the crewmen returned to MGB 318 declaring there was no sign of life on Rosservor – there was no one there to collect. The conditions were so bad that the crewmen hadn't even managed to unload the supplies for the Resistance.

Disheartened, the MGB weighed anchor and withdrew, knowing they would have to make another attempt, but just as they turned, they sighted two German trawlers coming across their bows. They stopped engines and waited. They didn't dare engage the enemy – that would have alerted the Germans to the postponed rendezvous. Apart from dropping a submarine sonar buoy to help with the navigation on the next mission, it had been a completely wasted journey.

Vital messages, it turned out, hadn't reached the French Resistance, so while MGB 318's boats were heading for a collection on Rosservor, the evaders had been huddled in the wet and cold on the nearby island of Guénioc. Days later they were still there waiting, hungry, disheartened, and suffering from exposure – the Germans had chosen to do their military exercises on the beach and the Resistance couldn't safely get them back to the mainland for a week.

Agent Maho managed to catch a lift on a Lysander airplane and in London discussed the situation with DDOD (I). Getting all the evaders out by plane would have been impossible – even if they could be moved across France, the Lysanders could only take a few at a time, and even the Lysanders were struggling with the weather. The sea was their only option and Maho desperately needed better radio contact and a supply of rubber dinghies to transport the evaders for the next pickup. On the night of 26 and 27 November, MGB 318 again left Falmouth, to drop off Maho and try again to collect the downed airmen.

Once again they reached the Aber Benoît estuary in poor visibility. The dinghies set out – but no one could be seen on Guénioc. In the end they dropped a seasick Maho on the mainland with a promise to try again, had a near miss on the rocks and, with engine trouble, crawled back to Falmouth. That was mission ENVIOUS II (a).

ENVIOUS II (b), unfortunately, was more of the same. After a difficult journey, they arrived at Guénioc island, but the evaders had not been able to get to Guénioc by boat and instead had managed to walk out on the strand to the islet of Tariec. Maho tried to get over to Guénioc in a canoe to tell the MGB 318 crew of their new location, but the weather was suddenly so bad that he just couldn't reach them. The three dinghies of MGB 318 were also suffering in the squall and were thought lost, hopefully stranded somewhere sheltered from the storm.

As MGB 318 weighed anchor, however, one of the rescue dinghies was spotted, caught by a reef and unable to row against the current to reach them. It was a moment of sheer terror for everyone as lines thrown to them were whipped back by the wind. The gunboat manoeuvred dangerously closer, dropping scrambling nets to the sinking dinghy – the dinghy's bung had been knocked out by rocks and crewman Lieutenant Uhr-Henry ruined his uniform cap frantically bailing out the rising water.

The crew and seven rescued evaders were pulled on board, only to suffer their worst crossing of the Channel. The stormy weather and ferocious sea caused the MGB to rock so violently that the lashing broke loose and sent heavy objects rocketing across the decks, threatening to injure those on board or damage the boat itself. Meanwhile, the persistent spray and water coming aboard completely soaked the maps and the equipment in the bridge. It was a wretched journey for all involved and particularly for David Birkin, the navigator who (already prone to seasickness) suffered terribly. Never had they been so pleased to see Falmouth.

Back in Guénioc the 'lost' members of the crew of MBG 318 had joined the evaders hidden by the French Resistance. Despite saving seven, numbers for the next attempt had swollen to twenty-four. Maho was desperately finding new hiding places amongst the local farms.

Another attempt was made in December 1943. This was operation FELICITATE and yet again the weather was appalling – everyone was so seasick that some members of the crew passed out. Needless to say it was another failure; it was becoming ever more obvious that they needed to find a better way through the surf.

On Christmas Day 1943 the weather suddenly started to improve. Here was their best chance of the winter and they took it. It was a last-minute arrangement, decided after everyone had finished their Christmas lunch, so David Birkin had to sober up fast to prepare the navigation charts. But the Germans wouldn't expect them on Christmas Day, would they? Radio contact with Maho suggested that the evaders were ready – if MGB 318 could just get close enough.

And something else was in their favour – they were joined by the team from Helford with their new 25-foot SN6 surfboat, designed by Nigel Warington Smyth. Skipper Howard Rendle, the coxswain, came aboard MGB 318, accompanied by six oarsmen specially trained for the SN6, among them Pip Jarvis.

The SN6 was the most advanced landing craft built by Nigel Warington Smyth and it had been tested by his experienced men in all conditions. She was clinker-built, i.e the hull planks overlapped, and the bow and stern were the same tapered shape to avoid having to turn the boat around onshore. Unlike a dinghy, she could also cope easily with small waves in shallow water and possessed well-secured oars made of rubber to muffle the sounds and for safety if the boat did capsize on top of them. The SN6 carried five passengers and emergency supplies as well as the three crew and would have been steered by the coxswain with a long sweep oar while two men rowed.

MGB 318 had not yet been fitted with lifting gear able to get the SN6 on board, so she was towed behind, easily coping in the gunboat's wake. On board there were additional dinghies and another surfboat, just in case. The weather stayed good and, as midnight approached, they were near Guénioc island, ready for the collection.

But what of the desperate fugitives? Would it be yet another failed attempt?

On Christmas Eve, the farmers around Aber Benoît gathered at the house of widow Pallier, bringing with them their hidden airmen and sailors, including two of MGB 318's crewmen, for a drunken celebration. Loudly they sang 'La Marseillaise' and 'Tipperary', a little risky as the Germans were just next door. But these people had been in hiding for such a long time – suffered cold, hunger and despair – that this was a brief escape for them. They even invited the German sentry in for a drink and, since they'd been there for so long, the sentry just thought they were the locals.

Twenty-four hours later, the local doctor called Marnière arrived in his ambulance, having secretly brought in those airmen hidden further afield. The ambulance got them safely through any German roadblocks. Some thirty-two individuals were going to embark on this attempt, including: MGB 318's crewmen lost in previous attempts, Maho's assistant, five other agents, two women, a French couple and sixteen aircrew. (There were definitely twenty-eight fugitives though accounts of their composition do vary.)

Approaching the beach in the dark, this was a large party to be hiding from the German sentries on the headlands above. Nonetheless, as they quietly made their way along cart tracks and across fields, they only attracted the attention of one barking dog. The beach had recently been mined by the Germans, but their guide, a farmer called Le Guen, had furtively watched the mines being placed. As they reached the beach, Le Guen dropped to his knees and carefully felt the ground in front of them – each buried mine left three antennae sticking up just an inch from the sand. Slowly feeling his way, he found a clear path to the shoreline and the evaders followed in the dark, each holding the shoulder of the person in front, their free hands holding pitchforks and rakes in case they had to fight off a German attack. A bizarre sight if anyone had been watching.

Finally the party followed the channels of seaweed which at low tide mark the strand to Tariec. Once there, they crouched behind the rocks and sandbanks, in the cold night air, waiting for the highly anticipated arrival of the boats.

And this time, at last, the boats arrived safely just after midnight. It was a moonless night, but oarsman Pip Jarvis could just make out the white waves lapping the shoreline. Leaving the gunboat near Guénioc, the SN6 surfboat easily and silently made it around to Tariec in twenty minutes – an 800-yard dash through surf over-looked by three enemy strongholds. Fifteen minutes later, they were back at the MGB 318, safely depositing their passengers and ready for another run. Assisted by the other surfboat on board, all crewmen and evaders were quickly collected, along with vital intelligence mail – great parcels of it.

Pip Jarvis must have been overjoyed that all that training on the Helford River had at last paid off. Aber Benoît had been difficult – the most difficult location they'd ever encountered – but it showed the Inshore Patrol Flotilla just what could be achieved with tenacity and ingenuity. Although many future operations shifted to the new MGBs at Dartmouth, Pip Jarvis continued at Helford until D-Day, training men in the new surfboats which would accompany every mission.

Sadly Agent Maho was captured before he could arrange the next pickup from Aber Benoît. He was severely tortured and sent to Dachau concentration camp, though he fortunately survived to be liberated by the Americans in 1945. Following his arrest, the German coastal searchlights intensified and the whole region was put on high alert. Interrogations and further arrests followed, with many farmers captured and killed for their part in the French Resistance, yet many of those remaining still helped to hide downed airmen and escaping prisoners of war. British Intelligence desperately needed another location for pickups ...

What of the mail Agent Maho was so desperate to deliver? It turned out to include the locations of the launch ramps for the V1 and V2 rockets bombarding London. Here at last were the targets the Allied bombers were looking for! General Eisenhower offered his congratulations to all the men involved in the missions to Aber Benoît while Pip Jarvis' commanding officer received an award for his inventions and went on to work for the Admiralty's Department of Miscellaneous Weapons Development (DMWD), known affectionately by the men as the 'Wheezers and Dodgers'.

Since 1940, the south coast of Britain had been a siege line, with the Germans increasingly on the attack from the western shores of France. In 1943, men like Pip Jarvis changed that – despite the increased German fortifications, they showed that the French coastlines could still be breached. Slowly the siege lines were shifting and very soon it would be the Nazis on the defensive.

After D-Day, June 1944, the base at Helford was scaled down and Pip Jarvis returned to coal mining in Newcastle. There was a shortage of skilled and experienced men in the mines and he knew he was needed back home, later working in the opencast coal mines. His son, Philip Jarvis, knew that his dad had spent the war in the navy, but it wasn't until Pip was very old that he told Philip that he'd been in the Special Service.

'Why did you never tell me before?' Philip asked his dad.

Pip Jarvis replied, 'I'd been told to keep it a secret.'

There are so many wonderful stories of the secret flotillas that I've had to be very selective and at times sadly leave some people out. If you would like to read more, I highly recommend Philip Jarvis' website: www.adept-seo. co.uk/inshore-patrol-flotilla. Philip is the son of Pip Jarvis of the Inshore Patrol Flotilla and he not only shared with me the stories on his excellent website but also let me use some of the photographs. He has many more terrific photos and diagrams on his website. Philip's Uncle Joe, Pip's older brother in the navy, was a signaller and was captured on film, with short clips here: www.youtube.com/watch?v=FBauqNpQAfY. It's terrific to hear the captain shouting for the signaller: 'Jarvis!'

I also recommend you take a look at Brook Richards' incredible and very detailed books on the secret flotillas (see References) – a monumental achievement. Pierre Hentic (Agent Maho) and others also have excellent biographies – sadly my French is just not good enough sometimes, so if anyone reading this is willing to translate these vital French stories into English so the English-speaking parts of the world can at last appreciate just how brave the French were during the Second World War, I will happily be your first customer!

JASPER LAWN'S
SECRET WAR

Jasper Lawn ended his days in a job he knew best, working the fishing boats off Fleetwood on England's north-west coast. He was a family man who adored his two grandchildren, Mark and Christopher. His two children, Sharon and Raymond, would often ask him about what he did in the war but he was a reticent man, unassuming, and, like many who had seen active service, he didn't like to talk about it.

Jasper Lawn in his navy uniform. (Reproduced with the kind permission of Jasper's daughter, Sharon Lawn)

Not even to his wife Peggy who was astonished when, after Jasper's death, she was invited to a fiftieth anniversary reunion at Flambards War Museum in Helston, Cornwall. A fiftieth reunion for what? She had no idea her husband had been such a major player in some of the most dangerous clandestine missions of the war.

Only when Jasper's widow read Sir Brook Richards' book *Secret Flotillas* did she discover her husband was a hero. Had she really known her husband at all?

It all started with a young Frenchman called Daniel Lomenech, who in September 1940, at the age of just 21, escaped with others from

Concarneau in France on a sailing boat called the *Lusitania*. They were picked up by a British trawler 20 miles off Penzance.

Daniel's parents ran a tunny fish-canning factory in Brittany so knew pretty much everything about French fishermen and the fishing grounds. When he joined the Royal Navy Volunteer Reserve and there met Sub-Lieutenant Steven Mackenzie, they quickly went looking for a suitable French vessel to re-establish contact with occupied France. A 65-foot Concarneau trawler called *Le-Dinan*, moored at Newhaven and registered as patrol boat N51, was exactly what they needed – perfect to sail near the French coast and collect intelligence packets and agents. The Breton's called her a *malamok*, used to catch the big tunny fish in the Atlantic. Her top speed was 6 knots, not very fast but perhaps fast enough.

N51 was soon fitted out, stripped of her guns, her masts restored, and sailed to Dartmouth. The converted fish hold became a wardroom for the crew and a special radio set was installed. Trial runs to the Scillies proved she needed a more resilient engine, so she was fitted with a British diesel engine with a higher horsepower, but still she wasn't capable of much more than 6 knots.

Jasper Lawn and the crew of N51. Left to right: Joe Houghton, Ronnie Rive, Jasper Lawn, Steven Mackenzie (behind) and Cookie Nash. (Reproduced with the kind permission of Jasper's daughter, Sharon Lawn)

Of course they needed a crew and Jasper Lawn was already working as a fisherman in Grimsby. He certainly looked the part – tough, stocky, a little weather-beaten, about 35, having been at sea around Hull and Grimsby since he was a boy. MacKenzie was full of admiration and certainly Lawn, although a man of few words, was a brilliant coxswain, able to negotiate the boat through rough seas.

They could have recruited some French fishermen but a lack of discipline had caused some concerns in Moreau's amateur adventures. Also, de Gaulle was determined that all French agents worked only for the Free French Secret Service – British Intelligence would have to find its own 'French people', often British who had grown up in France, or Canadians who spoke fluent French. There was often a disheartening lack of co-operation between the allies.

Recruits from the navy might have baulked at the cramped quarters, terrible working conditions and the constant stench of fish and diesel oil. Even MacKenzie couldn't stand the smell and preferred to brave the weather on deck. For British fishermen signing up for the war, however, it was another day 'at the office'.

From refugee French fishermen they 'borrowed' canvas trousers and smocks which made the N51's crew at least appear French. The men kept their uniforms and naval identity cards aboard in case they were captured, though in October 1942 Hitler would order that all Allied commandos should be shot on sight whether in uniform or not.

Jasper Lawn (left) and Joe Houghton. (Reproduced with the kind permission of Jasper's daughter, Sharon Lawn)

The crew of the N51. (Reproduced with the kind permission of Jasper's daughter, Sharon Lawn)

In case N51's crew had to resist a boarding party, there was a supply of Sten guns, grenades and pistols. An anti-tank rifle was also scrounged from the army – about enough firepower to stop the engine of any attacking German patrol boat – and they even staged a surprise attack on a local motor launch, with only the launch's captain knowing their intentions. Their success gave them confidence.

Meanwhile, Slocum (of British Intelligence) was desperately using submarines to rendezvous with agents off the coast of France but it was a dangerous business now that the Germans were on constant patrol and had battle cruisers stationed at Brest. British submarines couldn't get close to the shore and agents had problems meeting them at the right time out in deeper water. Could a fishing trawler do a better job? Of course it could, but Slocum didn't want any buccaneering adventurer like Holdsworth (*see* Chapter 8) doing the job. This had to be a bona fide navy operation.

Most important was establishing a secure mail run with Colonel Gilbert Renault, code name 'Rémy', who organised the extensive Confrérie de Notre Dame (CND) intelligence network for the Free French. Mackenzie and Lomenech were soon in London meeting Rémy to discuss the next pickup.

Rémy explained to them that he urgently needed to evacuate his wife and children from France as they were in danger of being captured by the Germans. It was March 1942 and the Germans were cracking down on the French Resistance – that siege line was moving back their way. Mackenzie and Lomenech discussed the arrangements, but at that stage could only offer collection by submarine; the details of N51 were still top secret and they weren't sure she would be ready in time. So they promised Rémy a Royal Navy pickup, but Rémy was going to be surprised (and delighted) by the 'Navy' vessel that appeared off shore.

Operation MARIE-LOUISE was scheduled for April 1942, with Mackenzie and Lomenech sailing N51 to the secluded New Grimsby Sound in the Scilly Islands as their point of departure. There N51 was given a false French registration number and painted in typically bright French colours. Getting the multicoloured paint from the local navy stores proved an adventure in itself: 'Well, you can have grey or … grey.'

Their first attempt was cancelled by Rémy but they set sail anyway just to 'test the waters'. Daniel Lomenech had been right – N51 fit in beautifully amongst the crabbers from Audierne and the trawlers from Le-Guilvinec. It was still early in the season for the Bretons' malamoks to be out fishing, but later they would see these glorious craft 'spreading blue, orange and white sails to the breeze as they came out of the islands heading for the broad Atlantic'. The N51 attracted so little attention that they might have been sailing in an English bay.

Scilly Islands, the point of departure for the N51. (Library of Congress, LC-DIG-ppmsc-08241)

Their second attempt in May 1942 was interrupted by an RAF attack on the port of Lorient. Rémy's small boat *Les-Deux-Anges* was undergoing repairs in Lorient Harbour when the RAF's mines closed the port. N51 again returned to the Scillies disappointed, though they did manage to get some supplies to 'postboxes' around Iles-Glénan.

A third attempt, on 16 June 1942, proved more dangerous, as Mackenzie described:

> We reached the position with half an hour in hand, and proceeded to steam up and down as though we were trawling ... A little after six, black smoke appeared on the southern horizon, quickly followed by the appearance of five German corvettes steaming up the convoy route towards us. We held our course, watching them anxiously, for they would pass all too close. Or would they pass? Was this a trap? Had Rémy been caught and our plans uncovered? As the corvettes came on, Jasper, the Coxswain, nudged my arm and pointed towards the islands. A tiny white sail had appeared there, too far off to identify but clearly making out to sea. The excitement grew intense; the corvettes lent the final touch of colour to the situation. We reached the end of our run and turned, letting them overtake us to starboard, between us and the islands. They passed us belching black smoke, the nearest less than a cable distant.

> We could see the Captain examining us through glasses on the
> bridge, watched the German sailors idling on deck: holding our
> thumbs we turned our backs on them. Then they were past, the casual
> inspection over.
>
> We watched the white sail tacking to and fro till the corvettes had
> disappeared. At last it steadied on a seaward course, making directly
> for us. We let it approach until we could identify it; everything fitted
> the description we held ... We made our signal, identified ourselves and
> went alongside.

Mackenzie peered down at the small trawler beside them, concerned to see only three fishermen on board – where were
Rémy's family? Then, to the amazement of the N51's crew, small
figures emerged from a multitude of secret hiding places in the
tiny boat: Rémy's wife, their three children (the youngest just 5)
another woman, a man with several suitcases and at last Rémy
himself, clutching a baby and a handful of papers. Just a little earlier,
the Germans had stopped and inspected *Les-Deux-Anges*, so it was
lucky everyone had been so well hidden.

The three fishermen received some supplies and, departing, spotted a German Heinkel flying overhead, but fortunately up too far to
have spotted the rendezvous. The crew of the N51 made gestures of
contempt at the Heinkel and set sail.

It was an emotional moment. Jasper Lawn was at the wheel, his
bright blue eyes gazing ahead, his voice gruffer when he spoke.
Crewman Cookie Nash had tears in his eyes as he watched the
retreating coastline.

A day later they were passing the Île de Sein when an armed patrol
came up to pass them portside. By sheer luck, the N51 was sitting
above a line of unattended trammel nets left there by earlier fishermen. As the patrol boat passed, N51's crew looked busy, hauling in
the nets and plucking out the spider crabs, just as the patrol's captain
checked them out, studying them carefully through his binoculars
from the bridge. It was a lucky escape and the spider crabs prepared
by Cookie Nash were delicious.

Then, about 10 p.m., as they were passing Brest, three German
destroyers approached starboard. As innocent French fishermen they
were making maximum speed northwards with dusk coming on –
conspicuously going in the wrong direction. One of the destroyers
broke away and headed for N51. The crew waited, terrified, unable

to do anything, when suddenly the destroyer turned and stopped. The crew set up the Lewis guns, just in case, but they could attack only if they reached British waters. However, the destroyer made no move to follow them. Another lucky break, and soon – at last – they were home.

As they approached the Scillies, a British gunboat appeared for the agreed rendezvous to transfer the passengers. To everyone's delight, the gunboat's loudhailer was belting out a Sousa march, a fittingly dramatic and uplifting end to a successful voyage.

They had saved Rémy and his family, but what of the vital intelligence papers? Rémy himself wasn't very enthusiastic about them. They were just some blueprints he'd found of the fortifications planned along the Normandy coastline; every wall, every blockhouse, every minefield, the calibre of the guns. German High Command didn't rate the Normandy plans of much importance either as they believed the Allies would try to invade somewhere further north, probably Calais.

Rémy declared to a friend in the Resistance: 'I shall send it to London, but I don't think it will be of any greater value than to show how the enemy conceive their Wall … it is better than nothing.'

Unknowingly Rémy and N51's crew had brought the Allied generals exactly the blueprints they needed for D-Day.

Lawn would continue as coxswain on many more voyages with Lomenech, and the fishing vessels were increasingly fitted with bigger engines, greatly increasing their speeds. Lomenech's second in command, Richard Townsend, became captain of his own ship, MFV 2022 or *Président-Herriot* and the 'mail runs' and missions to collect agents continued, through increasingly dangerous waters. In-between these difficult missions the crewmen appreciated a few shore comforts at the local pub, the New Inn, and Tresco's Land Girls are said to have particularly enjoyed the company of the good-looking Lomenech.

In 1943, the Land Girls were disappointed when Lomenech transferred to work on submarines, but Jasper Lawn would continue on board many of the ships of the Inshore Patrol Flotilla established in June 1943, working alongside Pip Jarvis' team (*see* Chapter 8). Under DDOD (I), the flotilla at Helford would comprise:

N51 – *Le-Dinan* or Motor Fishing Vessel (MFV) 2020

P11 – *Ar-Mouscoul* or MFV 2021

A04 – *Président-Herriot* or MFV 2022

L'Angèle-Rouge or MFV 2023

Fée-des-Eaux or MFV 2025

Sirène or MFV 2026, a converted 55-foot French crabber

Korrigan or MFV 2027, a 50-foot French trawler, Le Corre's old vessel from Le-Guilvinec (*see* Chapter 3)

L'Oeuvre or MFV 2028, a 65-foot French fishing vessel.

As well as two large trawlers:

105-foot *Breeze* and 106-foot *Jacques-Morgand*

Land Girls hard at work. (Library of Congress, LC-USE6-D-010008)

L'Angèle-Rouge, MFV 2023. (Reproduced with the kind permission of Jasper's daughter, Sharon Lawn)

A mission on the P11 *Ar-Mouscoul* to return Rémy to France in September 1942 revealed the increasing threats. The Germans, annoyed by the flotilla's successes, were now so stringent in their security checks that the French sailor who met them refused to take Rémy with him back to France.

The dangers did, however, have their lighter moments. Speed was still an issue, so yacht-designer Laurent Giles at Cowes built a high-speed hull with a French fishing boat superstructure for them. She was called *L'Angèle-Rouge* after Slocum's red-haired secretary who would soon become Mackenzie's wife.

On board *L'Angèle-Rouge*, one crewman's job was to burn cotton waste in a grate at the base of a dummy exhaust pipe, the thin smoke giving the appearance of them chugging along on a small diesel engine, masking their real horsepower and the powerful propellers. One day a German patrol appeared, distracting the crewman, who spilled the burning material and accidentally set fire to the deck in the wheelhouse. Easy to put out, but not without a huge amount of smoke. The German vessel came closer and the German captain enquired in impeccable French, 'Do you require assistance?' A very embarrassed crewman replied politely 'Non, merci' and the patrol boat went on its way.

On another occasion, Daniel Lomenech had to take *L'Angèle-Rouge* back to Cowes for an engine overhaul. They joined a convoy appropriate for their camouflage as a 6-knot fishing boat. Coming out of Yarmouth all the ships were lined up in order of naval seniority: the navy's Hunt class destroyer in front, then Lomenech as the Lieutenant Royal Navy Volunteer Reserve in *L'Angèle-Rouge*, followed by all the merchant ships. John Garnet, Lomenech's second in command, described what happened next:

> Coming up to Cowes, the Hunt class destroyer increased its speed because they wanted some leave that night. They went to 12 knots as did the little fishing vessel behind him. So he increased speed again – and so did the little fishing boat.
>
> Finally the Hunt went to 20 knots, and the fishing boat followed. The senior officer on the destroyer signalled to Daniel 'What's your maximum speed?' Daniel flashed back 'You would be surprised' and put her up to 28 knots, ran round the destroyer's bow and shot into Cowes.
>
> He had totally compromised the secret boat and there was talk of a court martial, but I expect – as usual – he got away with it …

These were also, of course, difficult missions frequently undertaken in stormy conditions. On Lawn's first mission with *L'Angèle-Rouge*, the drop was a success, but rough seas gave them their worst journey home. On another venture, *L'Angèle-Rouge* was 30 miles off Brest when a huge searchlight picked them out. They thought that a German destroyer had got them at last, but the crew had not yet heard of the British 'Leigh Light' Wellington bombers using radar to pick out German submarines on the surface before dropping depth charges. Fortunately the Wellington's pilot had looked first and seen it was a fishing boat, not a submarine. John Garnet described how 'the coxswain on watch never really recovered from that appalling experience!'

JJ TREMAYNE

JJ's real name was Jean-Jacques Gilbert. However, French naval officers who joined the Royal Navy after the fall of France were in danger and often condemned to death in absentia by court martial in France. They were also disliked by the Gaullists who believed that all French patriots should join the Free French Forces. So, on joining the Royal Navy, JJ was given a British surname and as JJ Allen he served on the Royal Navy Q-ship, HMS *Fidelity*.

Q-ships were the navy's version of a wolf in sheep's clothing. Pretending to be merchant ships, they were heavily armed, being designed to lure submarines and sink them. *Fidelity* was converted in September 1940 to carry a torpedo defense net, four 4-inch guns, four torpedo tubes, two Kingfisher float planes and Motor Torpedo Boat 105. She sailed with a French crew disguised as merchantmen, including JJ Allen.

In the early hours of 25 April 1941, HMS *Fidelity* (formerly a French Q-ship called the *Rhin*) landed two agents of the Special Operations Executive (SOE), a Pole and a Maltese, on a beach near the Étang de Canet on France's Mediterranean coast. On the return journey to *Fidelity*, the transporting skiff turned turtle in a squall and only one of the crewmen made it, swimming to the shore. A French police officer then arrested the crewman, who declared he was an evading Canadian airman called Patrick Albert O'Leary. Actually he was nothing of the sort; he was a Belgian doctor called Albert-Marie Guérisse and he would establish one of the most successful escape networks of the war (*see* Chapter 11). Later that same year, on 19 September, *Fidelity* disembarked an SOE team north of Perpignan on that same French coast. They were Robert Leroy, Raymond Roche, Francis Basin and Georges Dubourdin – all successful saboteurs and Resistance leaders, though sadly not all of them would survive the war.

On 30 December 1942, *Fidelity* was sunk by U-boat 435, killing most of the crew of 400, and JJ Allen was one of the few survivors. Recovering from his ordeal, he changed his name to Jean-Jacques Tremayne (still JJ to the crew) and replaced Lomenech as captain of *L'Angele-Rouge* in 1943.

Sub-Lieutenant Paul O'Brien had a good story about JJ Tremayne. He described how *L'Angele-Rouge* was fitted with two buckets hanging from a wooden gallows; when the buckets dragged in the water they were supposed to look like the ship was dragging nets, but of course they held nothing but water. On one trip, though, they were nearly caught out. They were chugging along off the Île de Sein, on their way home with two agents. It was a hot day, the water like a vast mirror, with every sound carrying for miles …

To the agents' disgust and ours a convoy of two submarines and several escorting heavy patrol boats, rather liked scaled-down destroyers, appeared dead ahead and steamed quite meaningfully towards us.

As we were trawling, to have altered course more than a little would have been a give-away to an alert observer, so we had to grin and bear it as they closed on us and passed no more than 200 yards off our starboard beam. A few minutes before this, there was a goose-pimply moment which pricked the euphoria of the agents we had just recovered. A flight of Junkers-88s swooped over us and released some shiny objects! Recognition signals for the subs, I hoped. So they proved, but the agents thought otherwise and dived under the nets secured along the gunwales. JJ advised them to stay there!

As the ships passed, they were so close we could see the faces of the crew, leaning over the rails, listening to some lugubrious German love-song. I was observing all this from the forrard hatch, partly hidden by the coaming. Good, I thought, they can't leave the convoy to ask for some fish – always a big worry because *Angele Rouge*'s buckets were a dead loss. This time, though, we had bought a deckload of fish from Newlyn, stowed in ice.

Just then, JJ in the wheelhouse suddenly put *Angele-Rouge* hard astern. There were literally clouds of smoke from the Hall-Scott's carefully hidden exhaust – not to mention churned-up water and spray! Surely, I thought, this is curtains. They can't ignore that – but they did. They must have had a good lunch. It turned out that JJ had spotted, just in time, a large Seine net only 50 yards ahead – and he had to keep our twin props clear of that, or else!

Ever so slowly, it seemed, the convoy drew away and a few hours later in the fading light we were on our way at a rate of knots.

The agents were still aggrieved. They had expected us to run for it – which would have been fatal. But JJ had done the right thing, and we were there to prove it.

But worse was yet to come. Just 30 miles off the Scilles, *L'Angèle-Rouge* was attacked by German aircraft. One of their two British Mustang escorts was knocked out of the sky and *L'Angèle-Rouge* was strafed with machine-gun fire. Lawn was terrified. The crewman beside him, his best friend, was killed and shrapnel hit Lawn in the face. His nose was scarred with a small hole mark for the rest of his life.

In February 1943, Jasper Lawn of the Royal Naval Patrol Service was awarded the Distinguished Service Medal for his work as coxswain on the N51, the P11 (*Ar-Mouscoul*) and *L'Angèle-Rouge*, and more medals would follow. Later, when peace came and Jasper headed to the Fleetwood fishing boats, the medals were all that his wife and family would know about his adventures.

On 24 May 1995, Jasper's wife Peggy, his daughter Sharon and Sharon's son Christopher (then 8 years old) attended the fiftieth reunion at Helston. Sadly it was five years too late for Jasper Lawn but many of Jasper's old friends from the war were there and

Colonel Rémy's medal, presented to Jasper Lawn's grandson Christopher at the fiftieth anniversary reunion in 1995. (Reproduced with the kind permission of Jasper's daughter, Sharon Lawn)

the Royal Navy marched to drums and trumpets. That evening, the family were invited with all the veterans for a meal at Nansloe Manor in Helston. First built as a sixteenth-century farmhouse, Nansloe Manor had developed into a grand manor with its own vast gardens and, during the Second World War, had served as a hospital for Italian and German prisoners of war.

During the meal, Jean Claude Renault, son of the famous French agent Rémy, turned to Richard Townsend and asked, 'Who's that little boy?' Townsend replied, 'That's Jasper's grandson.' Christopher was called over and Renault formally presented the boy with one of Rémy's medals in memory of Jasper Lawn, to whom Jean Claude Renault and his family owed their lives. It was a very proud moment for Peggy, Sharon and of course for young Christopher. If Jasper Lawn could had been there, he would have been happy that at last they could all share his secret.

The next day, the family were given a wonderful tour of the Helford River where Jasper had spent so much of the war. Back home, Jasper's story appeared in the local paper with the headline 'Fleetwood's Unknown Hero'. Jean Claude Renault kept in touch and sent Christopher a book; Rémy's autobiography called *Le Refus: Mémoire d'un Agent Secret de la France Libre.*

Jasper Lawn (on right) with navy friends. (Reproduced with the kind permission of Jasper's daughter, Sharon Lawn)

On 2 July 2000, a small group of Special Forces veterans stood in silence as former Sub-Lieutenant Paul O'Brien unveiled a plaque near Braiden Rock, the site of N51's mooring near New Grimsby Sound on Tresco. It was a simple but moving ceremony, attended by General Sir Michael Rose, Robert Crawford, the Director General of the Imperial War Museum, Sir Brook Richards and families of the officers and crewmen.

Paul O'Brien spoke warmly of their experiences:

> Of course the many missions would not have been possible without our marvellous crews. They were nearly all fishermen, and they were not only sea salts, but the salt of the earth as well. You could not fault any of them. I know that both Daniel Lomenech and Richard Townsend would like me to remember and savour especially Jasper Lawn, Ralph Hockney [their two coxswains] and Cookie Nash who kept us alive with his amazing meals, come hell or high water.
>
> If Braiden Rock marked our departure, it was also our point of return to the genuine warmth, hospitality and kindness of the people of Tresco. Above all, we would like to thank and salute them for keeping 'mum' for so long and so successfully!
>
> I know the crews would have liked me to mention without fail John Williams of the New Inn and his wife who did so much to sustain their morale!
>
> Thus the plaque I will now unveil – it is not only for the ships, but will be a lasting memento and symbol of the continuing bond between us, our friends here, and all Scillonians.

At last Jasper Lawn's secret war was no longer a secret.

Sharon Lawn, Jasper Lawn's daughter, was very generous, offering photos and sharing her memories of her father – thank you to Sharon and her brother Raymond Lawn. Any mistakes are definitely mine. John Davies-Allen kindly sent me the archived articles from www.islandrace.com (sadly no longer active). I understand the Isles of Scilly Museum has an excellent exhibition about the secret flotillas, and I hope someday to get the chance to visit.

CROSSING
THE CHANNEL

The train from London travelled along the shore to Kingswear, across the river from the hills of Dartmouth with its clusters and rows of white houses. Gunboats and torpedo boats by the quaysides were shrouded in sea mist as the train pulled into the riverside station next to the Royal Dart Hotel.

As the passengers stepped out on to the railway platform, a few of the travellers (dressed in European clothing and carrying strange parcels) made their own way silently on to the ferry and across the

Kingswear, where many agents would begin their journey.
(Library of Congress, LC-DIG-ppmsc-08273)

Dartmouth and Kingswear. (Author's collection)

River Dart to the old paddle steamer called *Westward Ho!* David Birkin watched these agents begin their journey. Hours later, they would be arriving in darkness on a French beach, scrambling ashore to meet the Resistance.

In 1942, Birkin was just Slocum's messenger boy between the office in London and the Naval Intelligence Division's growing gunboat flotilla at Dartmouth, but Birkin became fascinated with the clandestine operations to and from France and begged his boss to be part of their missions. The Medical Board, however, had pronounced David Birkin unfit for any form of military service – he suffered from seasickness, was prone to sinus infections, had bleeding lungs and double-vision. After two years of working as a telegraphist, spending most of that time in hospital for sinus and eye operations, Birkin had dwindling hopes of ever seeing the 'real' war. Working for Slocum, head of transport operations for the British Intelligence Services, was the best he could hope for. Or so he thought.

The 15th Motor Gunboat Flotilla at Dartmouth urgently needed navigators to get them to the French coast and surprisingly Slocum was willing to let David Birkin have a go, sending him on a crash course in navigation and assigning him on probation to Motor Gunboat 318 – the only gunboat available to them at that time – while they waited for MGBs 501, 502 and 503 to turn up (*see* Chapter 8). Meanwhile, the Germans were still dropping bombs along the

River Dart, attacking Noss shipyards and the Naval College – twenty-five people were killed on 18 September 1942 and another fifteen in 1943 when bombs fell on Duke Street and Higher Street.

While David Birkin was in training, Pierre Guillet was sent from the Helford Flotilla (*see* Chapter 8) to help with navigation on MGB 318. Pierre was not his real name but a name he'd assumed to protect his family back in France. He was an experienced French tunny fisherman who'd previously sailed round Cape Horn in a square-rigged ship, his experience granting him the ranking of lieutenant. He knew the Brittany coastline better than anyone and he'd already helped Holdsworth disguise the *Mutin* as a French fishing vessel.

Pierre turned up in Dartmouth happy to help the British, but Slocum's man Ted Davis, an officer of MGB 318, took one look at the scruffy fisherman in his mid-50s standing on the quayside in his duffel coat and asked, 'What is that?' When someone explained to Davis that Pierre was an experienced navigator and French fisherman, Davis declared loudly, 'I was navigating officer of the *Queen Mary* when she did a world cruise and I don't need a stupid fisherman to tell me where I am.' Ah, the hubris …

Davis then set out aboard MGB 318 to deliver supplies to the Resistance and became dangerously lost in the bad weather – four times. It seemed that whichever their course, they were stopped by rocks or white water. The SOE demanded to know why their expert navigator Pierre Guillet could not pinpoint the target location, only to be informed that Pierre had never been allowed on board.

Dartmouth, Royal Naval College. (Author's collection)

On the fifth attempt, Pierre walked up to Davis on the bridge and declared, 'Me go this time'. Davis agreed, but then Pierre argued, 'If me go this time, then you f… off ashore. If you go, me f… off ashore.' Insubordination left Pierre standing on the quayside, while Davis failed again to find the target.

On his return after another failure, things were looking desperate, so Davis was suddenly and unexpectedly 'called to London for an urgent meeting' and Letty, the second-in-command, took over, taking Pierre Guillet with him on MGB 318 on 10 November 1942. They found the correct beach straight away, proving that Pierre knew that coastline better than anyone, but Pierre was urgently needed back at the Helford Flotilla base. Would David Birkin, the new navigator, ever manage to do as well as Pierre? Could Birkin now get them safely to France?

On his first time aboard, Birkin came rushing down a ladder and stepped on the commanding officer's fingers – he thought that was the end of his probation, but his punishment was just a volley of expletives. When it came to navigation, though, Birkin was quick to learn and soon had the expertise they so urgently needed. Their charts for the rock-infested north Brittany coast were out of date and using radar would attract unwanted attention from the enemy, so Birkin had only a compass, logbook and an echo-sounder to find their way in the pitch dark and, after steaming across the Channel for seven hours, the echo-sounder often didn't work.

Obviously they needed to set some navigational buoys and Birkin was tasked with fitting them with self-destruct charges, just in case they were discovered by the Germans. The weather off the Brittany coast was atrocious – real January weather for the Channel – and Birkin set out from MGB 318 in stormy seas, accompanied by an ageing rating who'd been called back out of retirement. Pounded by waves, they worked with 4 pounds of TNT, detonators, a DIY assembly diagram and a rusty penknife. They got the job done. That was his first mission.

In MGB 318's chart room, every mission was a challenge. The bridge might have been armoured, but the chart room was just plywood, as Birkin discovered when the boat lurched and he fell through the wall. The chart-table was collapsible (as it frequently demonstrated) and in the diffused lighting, red for blackout purposes, he could barely see the charts. To add to the discomfort, the room stank of cabbage and engine oil, and from the voice-pipe connecting him with the bridge came seawater and rust, often pouring through in foul weather. When the ship first nosed into the swell, David Birkin was up to his ankles in salt water, trying to read sodden charts; the lamp exploded on the floor and in the sudden darkness, he was violently sick. Only another twenty-three hours of similar conditions to go …

Despite this, Birkin proved his brilliance. Every rock at various tides along the French coast was painstakingly charted, so Birkin could instantly tell the commanding officer what to look out for, what to avoid and, perhaps more importantly, exactly where they were. Outwardly confident, Birkin was always secretly worried that any miscalculation could shatter the hull at any moment.

In 1942, MGB 318 was the only gunboat readily available to Slocum. Most of the runs across the Channel had to be done by fishing boat (*see* Chapters 8 and 9). But in 1943, French agent Rémy's lines from France broke down under the barrage of increased German security. The fishing boats flotillas from Falmouth and Helford (*see* Chapters 8 and 9) were suddenly redundant and alternative routes had to be established urgently.

MGB 318 continued to work alone – including the Aber Benoît mission (*see* Chapter 8) – until early 1944, when MGB 502 and 503 and others were assigned to Slocum, now Deputy Director Operations Division (Irregular). At last the 15th MGB Flotilla was formed. During 100 successful missions they rescued over 150 agents, downed airmen and fugitives from the shores of France.

FRANÇOIS MITTERRAND

On the night of 25/26 February 1944, MGB 502 set out from Dartmouth to the French beach code-named L'Atelier, under the Beg-an-Fry headland west of Roscoff and Carantec. They were to land two agents and collect a group of ten. Those embarking waited nervously on the beach – a previous attempt had failed, but this time they heard 502's engines stop and surfboats heading towards them.

The missions were now following a strict routine based on experience. Radio contact was first made with the group leader onshore and then the first surfboat would set off, carrying an armed lookout on its bows. The group leader onshore would identify him or herself to the first boat by agreed code name. The two agents followed in the second surf-boat, wearing gas-capes over their clothes which prevented any telltale stains from the sea water. The agents were then carried to the shore to keep their feet dry, before the gas-capes were collected and taken carefully back to the surfboat. There would be no communication between those disembarking and those waiting on the shore to embark. No one was allowed hats or headgear of any sort in case it blew off, leaving traces of their presence for Germans to find.

Those embarking were treated like luggage – staying seated until the last moment they were brought over to the surf-boat. The whole mission was supposed to take three or four minutes, but fog delayed the embarkation at L'Atelier and MGB 502 stayed perilously close to shore for three and a half hours. The radio they were using, an American-made S-phone, developed a fault and the shore team in the fog had to signal MGB 502 using torches at sea level. The ship's bow that approached was at first thought to be German but as the scrambling nets were dropped over the side, the shore team realised with great relief that they were safe to embark.

They arrived back at Kingswear at last and, in the early hours, the first train at the station heading for London waited for an extra few minutes as a group of exhausted civilians boarded and drew the blinds in their reserved compartment. Just hours before they had been 100 miles away, under the noses of German lookouts, dangerously close to the Gestapo headquarters at Morlaix.

One of the agents delivered to Beg-an-Fry was François Mitterrand. From the beach he was escorted to the house of a retired police officer at Kergariou. Later he was safely driven to Doctor Le Duc's house at Morlaix and from there he boarded a train to rejoin the French Resistance. He left his ration card with Madame Le Duc, written in his code name, Morland.

Mitterrand was lucky. Only three nights later, at the same beach, MGB 502 dropped off a Corsican agent called Defendini who was captured soon after his arrival and died in Buchenwald concentration camp in September 1944.

François Mitterrand had enlisted in the French Army and was badly wounded and then captured in June 1940. He remained a prisoner of war for eighteen months in Germany until at last, after many attempts, he managed to escape and join his hero Marshall Pétain in Vichy France. Even in Vichy France there were resistance movements, all the more active after the Germans invaded in November 1942, and Mitterrand's network of resistance fighters battled the Germans throughout the war.

However, Mitterrand and General de Gaulle would never see eye to eye. Mitterrand distrusted de Gaulle's determined rise to power and his demands to control all of the French Resistance inside and outside France. Not everyone wanted to join the Free French Forces. De Gaulle, meanwhile, distrusted Mitterrand for his time in Vichy France and saw prisoners of war as unpatriotic, failing to uphold the fight against the Nazis. De Gaulle demanded patriotism; Mitterrand sought understanding and compassion.

While Mitterrand passed through Dartmouth, de Gaulle's son Philippe was serving around Dartmouth with the 23rd Motor Torpedo Boat Flotilla of the Free French Forces. Charles de Gaulle would be President of France from 1959 until 1969, and his son would become inspecteur-general of the French Forces. From 1981 until 1995, François Mitterrand would be President of France.

LA CHATTE

Mathilde Carré, known as La Chatte (The Cat) had been a senior agent in the Interallié network, flirting with the Germans in Paris and then sending information to London. When Interallié was betrayed, La Chatte was arrested and, unknown to British Intelligence, avoided torture by agreeing to be a double agent for the Germans. Another agent in France, code-named 'Lucas', was introduced to La Chatte and told that she was someone who could get messages for him to London, but Lucas quickly realised she was a German spy.

The story goes that La Chatte confessed and Lucas convinced her to work again for the Allies as a triple agent, but subsequent events make this a strange bargain: to get La Chatte and himself to England, Lucas made a deal with the Germans. Had they in fact both sold out to the enemy? Lucas and La Chatte agreed with the Nazis that, pretending to be Allied agents, they would arrange to be collected by the British on the north coast of Brittany while the Germans watched. Perhaps Lucas thought this was the only chance of getting him and La Chatte back to England. It seemed to be a flawed plan and in fact the Germans had set a very effective trap.

On the night of 11/12 February 1942, MGB 314 journeyed from Dartmouth to Locquirec (west of Lannion in France) to drop off agents Abbott and Redding, and collect Lucas, La Chatte and another SOE officer, Ben Cowburn, who had just successfully sabotaged an oil refinery. Abbott and Redding landed safely with Ivan Black, the MGB 314's Australian First Lieutenant in charge of the landing. But as they prepared to return, the sea got rough. As Lucas climbed into the dinghy, it capsized, sending La Chatte into the surf. Lucas dragged La Chatte from the water, dripping in her fur coat and spitting with fury as her luggage disappeared.

The five stranded agents quickly separated but the watching Germans were just as quick to round them up. Ivan Black was in his uniform and was treated as a prisoner of war. Abbott and Redding were hiding in a barn when the farmer gave them up and Lucas persuaded the Germans to treat the pair as prisoners of war as well – they were sent to Colditz. Ben Cowburn was tailed for miles but, being an accomplished agent, he managed to give them the slip and headed for Spain.

British Intelligence, knowing nothing of these captures, still expected to have to collect Lucas and La Chatte and so another attempt was made on 13 February, again failing because of the surf. Further attempts were made, this time at Pointe-de-Bihit north of Lannion on 20 and again on 22 February, but La Chatte and Lucas weren't there. Again the British tried, this time on 27 February, again at the Pointe-de-Bihit, and at last Lucas and La Chatte were brought back successfully to Dartmouth.

But it was all for nothing. Having travelled by train from Kingswear, Lucas announced in London that he'd brought back a triple agent and La Chatte was treated like a queen. But she didn't realise her hotel room was bugged. The result? La Chatte spent the rest of the war in prison and Lucas was arrested as a traitor for making a deal with the Germans.

A QUIET OCCUPATION?

As France fell to the Germans, authorities on the Channel Islands were giving the British citizens there mixed messages about the need to evacuate. The Governor of Jersey and his wife fled on the *Philante* on 21 June 1940, but when the *Sabre* arrived later the same day, only about 8,000 people were willing to be evacuated from Jersey and only half the population from St Peter Port on Guernsey.

On 30 June 1940, five German planes landed on Guernsey. To the Islanders, the German soldiers were surprisingly pleasant, at least at first. For the Germans, this seemed like a picturesque location to sit out the war. The German occupation of the Channel Islands had begun.

In the early days, Winston Churchill was determined to get the Channel Islands back, particularly because the German occupation sent morale in mainland Britain plummeting. But the first attempts were embarrassingly unsuccessful.

On 6 July 1940, Second Lieutenant Hubert Nicolle, a Guernsey man, boarded a submarine at Devonport equipped with just a canoe. Preparations had been so rushed that his canoe didn't fit through the hatch on the submarine and a replacement had to be found in a hurry. Eventually Nicolle was landed in Guernsey for reconnaissance duties. Three days later, two other men from Guernsey, Philip Martel and Desmond Mulholland, were deposited on Guernsey and Nicolle was picked up. All this was part of the preparation to decimate the Germans.

On 14 July 1940, three launches were sent to Guernsey with an invading force of 140 men. They believed it would take just one hour and forty minutes to take back the island. One launch went in the wrong direction, another sprang a leak, the third landed at Jerbourg but there were no Germans there. In the end, the three launches returned having achieved nothing, failing even to collect Martel and Mulholland.

Guernsey. The Channel Islands were occupied by the Germans between June 1940 and May 1945. (Library of Congress, LC-DIG-ppmsc-08103)

Jersey. Prior to occupation the Germans attacked the Island from the air, killing nine and wounding many. (Library of Congress, LC-DIG-ppmsc-08118)

The response from the Germans was devastating – as punishment, they cracked down on the population, searching for agents in their midst. The Island's authorities accused the raiders of upsetting what had so far been a peaceful (if unwanted) occupation, and many Islanders worried that their sons, serving with the British Forces, might be sent in the next raid. Martel and Mulholland eventually gave themselves up through the Guernsey authorities and fortunately were treated as prisoners of war rather than secret agents, which would have meant the death sentence.

In September 1940, Hubert Nicolle was returned to Guernsey with James Symes to survey the fortifications. Nicolle and Symes turned up at the farm of Nicolle's old school friend Tom Mansell, who gave them a tour of gun emplacements while delivering his milk round. Bad weather prevented their return and the two agents were forced into hiding for six weeks, all the while terrified they were putting their relatives and friends in danger. Their friends found them uniforms which helped give them the appearance of military officers and they turned themselves in to the Germans. But this time the Germans denounced them as spies, had them court-martialled and sentenced to death. Thirteen of their friends and relatives were captured, including the head of Guernsey's government who had been aware of the agents' presence on the Island, and all civilian radios were confiscated.

Oberst Graf von Schmettow had recently arrived to take charge of the German soldiers on the Island, and took the prisoners' case to Berlin, where it was decided that they were guilty but the Germans would be merciful and no one would be executed. The agents were again treated as prisoners of war and their friends and family were released. Sadly, the agent James Symes' father, trapped in a French prison for two months awaiting the verdict, had already slashed his wrists and was found dead in his cell. Once more the Guernsey Government blamed Britain for putting them all in danger by sending local boys in the raids.

Channel Islanders were in an unusual situation: the flawed evacuation had separated many from their children, and a number had sons in the British Forces, yet many of the German soldiers were young and homesick and would do anything to be invited into someone's house for tea. These friendly Germans would also smuggle in food to help the struggling Islanders, although fraternisation was frowned upon. One Islander reported someone's son for being seen in the company of two Germans, absurdly failing to notice the lad was handcuffed to the Germans at the time. Island men were recruited into building watchtowers and fortifications and British airport workers were dismayed to watch German bombers leave the runways, headed for England. By the end of 1940, the front page of the *Guernsey Evening Press* was announcing Britain's imminent collapse.

The Jersey Lighthouse. (Library of Congress, LC-DIG-ppmsc-08138)

Royal Navy Submarine HMS A6. (Author's collection)

During 1940, sixty people escaped Guernsey for England and the result was heavy regulations against fishing boats going out in fog or rain – if the weather worsened, boats had to return to port immediately. All ports were mined and, after an escape from Guernsey in 1943, fishing and all access to beaches were banned. For the Germans, this 'iron hand in velvet glove' policy was a rehearsal for their invasion of England; the increasing need for punishments reveal it was a flawed policy.

Now the Islanders felt abandoned by Britain, left hungry and isolated. The Allies had decided against a major attack which, in such heavily populated islands, would result in civilian casualties, but the lack of any major attempt to reclaim the Islands gave Hitler some false hope that Britain was an easy target and would soon be successfully invaded, that Britain did not have the resources for any major fightback into Europe. An incredible proportion of German resources were concentrated on fortifying the Channel Islands, making it the most heavily defended occupied territory on the French coastline. However, this was actually beneficial for the British Forces – while the Germans diverted men and major supplies to the Islands, the British could attempt landings along the French coast a little more easily. The Channel Islands sadly had to be sacrificed for the war effort.

But there were still attempts to help the Islanders. In 1940, there were five failed attempts to land small British forces on the Islands and then, on 2 September 1942, the Casquets Lighthouse off Alderney was captured from the Germans, with eight German prisoners taken. The raid was led by John Newton, a Guernsey fisherman and notorious smuggler, renowned for his 'buccaneering spirit'; in other words an untrustworthy villain in peacetime with just the sort of bravado that the mission required (*see* Chapter 8). When the Channel Islands were under threat of invasion back in June 1940, the leaders of Guernsey had sent a telegram to the British Admiralty asking if John Newton might be relieved of his navy duties and sent back to them – he was, they felt, their only hope of smuggling food into the Islands when the Germans invaded. Sadly, John Newton could not be found before the Germans took control of Guernsey and instead Newton was recruited to work for the secret flotilla at Helford.

John Newton was assigned to lead the mission for the Small Scale Raiding Force (SSRF), an organisation based in Poole, as they captured the lighthouse off Alderney. The SSRF achieved some remarkable results and, although most members of the SSRF were eventually killed or captured, the organisation would go on to become the highly effective amphibious section of the Special Boat Squadron (SBS). However, in 1942, the Casquets Lighthouse was impossible to defend and was quickly retaken.

In October 1942, a twelve-man raiding party landed on Sark only to meet disgruntled Islanders, disappointed that King George VI's radio speeches had made no mention of their plight. The raiding party killed two Germans and took another back to Britain as a prisoner. However, the consequences were horrific. Hitler heard how the German prisoner's hands had been tied and retaliated by having 1,376 Allied prisoners at Dieppe shackled. One Sark woman had helped the British raiders so Hitler had 200 Islanders deported to internment camps on the mainland and ordered that all commandos – brutal animals in Hitler's view – should, in future, be shot on sight. The SSRF would lose a high proportion of its small numbers executed by the Nazis and the Germans were even ordered to shoot unarmed captives.

Raids in 1943 faced opposition from the terrified Islanders, refusing to help the British men for fear of reprisals. Soon the British realised that the Islanders wanted nothing to do with them.

There were pockets of resistance in the Channel Islands, though no one in the British Government would hear much about them until well after the war. In 1943, a driver for the Nazis escaped with all their plans. Despite the food shortages, the Islanders – even children – made desperate and dangerous attempts to feed the starving Russian and Jewish prisoners brought into the Islands to construct the fortifications.

One Jersey Islander, Albert Bedane, was awarded a gold watch from the Russians for his wartime resistance efforts and would eventually be posthumously declared 'Righteous Among the Nations' by the Israelis.

Albert had grown up on Jersey and, married with a daughter, he ran a physiotherapy clinic in St Helier that was frequented by the German soldiers. Unknown to the enemy, the three-room cellar beneath them was being used to hide an escaped French prisoner of war, three Russian slave workers and, for two and a half years, Mrs Mary Richardson who had escaped being sent by the Germans to a 'nice special camp'. Throughout the war, when the German officers asked about his Jewish wife, Mr Richardson feigned senility.

For more stories of the 15th MGB Flotilla, please see Brook Richards' excellent book Secret Flotillas. *I also rather like Porter's book* Frank Jones and the Secret War *with some wonderful first-hand accounts of working in Dartmouth and Kingswear. Madeleine Bunting's book on the Channel Islands is also recommended reading.*

ESCAPE
FROM DIEPPE

The story of the most audacious escape line between the French coast and south-west England begins with the disastrous Allied invasion attempt at Dieppe, with a French-Canadian commando called Lucien Dumais desperately trying to escape the German gunfire.

The landing craft had gone and the inferno on the beach was getting worse. Enemy tracer fire intersected the 200 yards ahead of them – nobody was going to go straight through that and live. Lucien Dumais spotted the casino about 35 feet to his right and signalled to his men to follow him. On route he met his platoon commander barely alive, both thighs bleeding on to the sand. The commander put Dumais in charge and Dumais slowly dodged his way under fire to the casino. He glanced back at the dwindling numbers following his path. Soon there wouldn't be many of his men left able to fight.

This was Dieppe in August 1942, a fruitless first attempt by the Allied Forces to see if they could invade the mainland via beach landings. Overwhelmed by German forces, 3,367 Allies servicemen were killed, wounded or captured – 68 per cent of the invasion force.

Dumais managed to defend their position from the casino building near the beach, but it was an impossible task, a brutal bloody mess, trying to survive until the evacuation boats appeared. Forced to leave the unconscious wounded behind, Dumais valiantly battled to get one wounded man out on to the nearest British boat now

40 yards from the shore. As Dumais then struggled to heave himself aboard, his waterlogged pack pulled him back into the water. Unable to wait, the boat was forced to make a hasty retreat leaving Dumais floundering in the waves, drowning under the weight of his own equipment. By some miracle his head was out of the water when he came to – he was on the beach but not out of danger.

As the British ships departed under heavy shelling, Dumais rallied the remaining men to defend their position, but surrounded only by the wounded and the exhausted, he knew their position was hopeless. Reluctantly Dumais ordered the surrender.

The Germans marched the prisoners for hours from town to town, the only provisions coming from kind French inhabitants who could do little more than look on as the prisoners swelled in number to over 1,500. Only now did Dumais realise the extent of the failure of the operation: Dieppe had been a disaster. Even so, the French people cheered the Allied soldiers for their attempt as the prisoners were herded through a station on to cattle trucks.

As the train travelled across France, Dumais and others managed to dislodge a plank barring one of the windows. As the track curved, putting the window out of sight of the German guards, three of the prisoners including Dumais managed to climb out on to the buffers but the train was moving too fast for them to jump off safely. Through two stations the three prisoners frantically clung on to the outside of the train – a bizarre sight for those standing on the platforms but surprisingly no one raised the alert.

Finally the train began to climb and slow down and the three made their jump, suddenly finding themselves under fire and making a terrifying run for the forest.

In the trees, Dumais lost his companions and discovered himself alone in occupied France. He planned to make for the coast and steal a boat back to England. He knew many French had made that journey in 1940 and thought it likely to succeed, but in training the men had been advised by the intelligence officers that if they were separated, they should make their way home via neutral Spain. That meant a 1,000-mile journey on foot. Or a train journey if he could find the money. He wasn't going to make it without some help.

The bedraggled man who appeared on Madame Collai's doorstep was no surprise. She'd heard about the Dieppe raid over the radio and had previously helped others escape the Germans. Escaped prisoners were only to be expected, but could Dumais trust Madame Collai?

At first he didn't think so, as she hid him in a locked cellar and disappeared. Had she gone to tell the Germans that she'd captured an escaped soldier? He quickly changed his mind as she returned, offering food, clothes to make him look like a French peasant, what money she could spare and temporary accommodation in a shack in the woods. She was putting herself in terrible danger and they both knew it.

Soon he was on a train to Poitiers and on his way to the border with Vichy France. He was travelling without papers and only a series of lucky escapes helped him avoid detection; the station gates were not always manned and he managed to leave the station at Poitiers without being stopped.

From there it was a long walk south to Limoges and the border. On the way he stopped at a blacksmiths to ask the lady there for a glass of water. This was his first big mistake – a French peasant would ask for wine. The lady frowned and warned him against travelling further south. It wasn't safe with German and French guards everywhere, determined to catch anyone illegally crossing the border. She invited him in, to sit until nightfall when the journey might be safer. As Dumais sat at her table, he decided he should tell her the truth and she stood speechless at his story, then disappeared to fetch her husband, the blacksmith.

Dumais glanced at the door, ready to flee if necessary but his fears were unfounded. The blacksmith rushed in to shake Dumais' hand, thrilled to hear of the attempted invasion and astonished that an escaped prisoner had managed to travel 250 miles through France as yet undetected. The blacksmith offered to take Dumais to the border, but Dumais was reluctant to risk this man's life.

Given detailed information about the border patrols, Dumais made ready to continue his journey on foot when a cart turned up outside driven by an old local man accompanied by his grandson. A coincidence? The blacksmith talked quietly to the old man and it was decided – the man would take Dumais on his cart as far as possible. It would be safer for Dumais to travel in company.

But what silent company it was. The old man said not a word for miles and then, in the middle of nowhere, stopped the horse on the road and indicated that Dumais should get out.

'There's the ditch,' the old man said in French, his first words all night as he pointed to the woods. 'Follow it as far as that field of Jerusalem artichokes. Take cover and don't move before nightfall. You'll be in full view of the Boche. When it's dark enough, make for that wood over yonder.'

The old man set off again, leaving Dumais to face the rest of his journey alone. Night fell and, as instructed, Dumais set out from his hiding place, keeping the moon to his left so he wouldn't get lost amongst the farmhouses and orchards. He moved silently, praying that he wouldn't awaken any dogs while, risking detection, he stole some fruit from the trees.

At last he was at the railway line that ran east to west separating the two zones: to the north occupied France, to the south Vichy France where conditions weren't much better but there were fewer Germans. Here at last was the border he'd travelled so far to reach. His first impulse was to rush across, but he checked himself – the border patrols might sit in wait for escapees just like himself. He surveyed the bushes either side, listening intently for any sign of life, sniffing the air for cigarette smoke that might indicate a sentry. Nothing.

He leaped over the fence, ran across the ballast, dived over the next fence into the bushes, and stopped again. The only sound he could hear was his own heart thumping. He was finally over the border. He made for the road, overjoyed and relieved, marching south at a brisk pace, only to be confronted by a guard shouting 'Halt!'

But Dumais was not going to stop now. Whether the guard was French or German, he didn't wait to find out. He took a few cautious steps back as the guard raised his rifle, then dived into the bushes and made a dash for it, as best he could through undergrowth that needed his knife to cut his way through. More guards, then the sounds of dogs – he still didn't stop. He'd been a good cross-country runner at his old base camp and he set himself in motion. He went 5 miles before even thinking of slowing down and then, when he felt it was safe, found himself a haystack to hide in for the night.

Another lucky escape but there was more than luck on his side. As morning came he set off down the road, hands in pockets, head down inconspicuously, when suddenly a car drew up beside him before he'd even heard it, let alone had chance to hide. The lady passenger wound down the window and casually asked him if he'd like a lift to Lussac-les-Chateâux.

He was miles from anywhere, so it was awkward to say no and the couple seemed straightforward people, though how he judged that is a mystery. During the ride, the woman was chatty, but the man driving kept glancing in the rear-view mirror at Dumais, suspicious it seemed of this strange traveller on the road. They stopped outside a garage in Lussac and let him out.

The driver leaned out of the window and asked Dumais, 'Would you be going to the Hotel de la Gare?'

Where had Dumais heard that name before? Someone had told him recently that once he was over the border he should look out for the Hotel de la Gare – of course, the blacksmith. Had the blacksmith phoned ahead and arranged all this to help him?

Of course it could be a coincidence so Dumais was cagey in his response. 'Not particularly,' he replied, 'unless the cooking is good.'

'The cooking is exceptionally good,' the man replied with a smile, 'you should try it.' Dumais was grateful for directions and, as the couple drove away, he realised that 'a whole conspiracy had been formed to help me on my way, and a wave of gratitude towards all these brave and friendly folk swept over me'. As the war progressed, many escapees travelling through France would know how he felt at that moment. Others, sadly, would not be so lucky.

The hotel, it turned out, was a base for the local Resistance and he was forced to wait while they made arrangements to get him to Marseilles. At first he was frustrated by the wait, until the French police knocked on the hotel's door at 2 a.m. He hurried to hide on the roof, peering over the gutters, only to realise that it wasn't him they were after. Instead he witnessed the true horror of occupied France. First he heard a woman screaming, then watched helplessly as the police dragged a Jewish woman and her 7-year-old son out into the street and took them away. There was nothing anyone could do but Dumais would be haunted by the woman's screams for the rest of his life. The Vichy police were arresting Jewish citizens who had previously made their way into the 'Free Zone' and sending them to a camp back at Poitiers to be handed over to the Germans. The French people were only now witnessing the true face of Vichy France – their armistice came with a price.

Suddenly Dumais' extended wait at the hotel did not seem so bad.

October 1942 and cold weather arrived before Dumais was on a train to Marseilles, accompanied by two French soldiers on their way to join the Free French Forces in England. There was still an American consulate at Marseilles and Dumais arrived there with his French friends, announcing he was an American citizen wanting to return home. The consul listened to his story, expressionless, and then declared that as Dumais was in fact Canadian and the USA was a neutral country in the war, there was nothing the consul could do. Goodbye.

Marseille, where Lucien Dumais would ask the American consul for help. (Author's collection)

Bitterly disappointed, Dumais ate lunch with his French colleagues in Marseilles, where they encouraged him to try the consul again without them. Perhaps their presence had made the consul less than helpful? Dumais tried again alone and this time the consul quietly told Dumais to pretend he had a sore throat and a sore right foot and present himself to this particular doctor at this address, but not to tell his French friends anything about it.

'Doctor, I have a sore throat and a sore right foot,' Lucien Dumais duly informed the doctor.

'Who sent you?' the doctor asked.

'The American Consul.' And that was it. Suddenly Dumais was out through a back door and introduced to Pat O'Leary who also promised to do what he could for Dumais' French friends. Dumais was now a package on the Pat Line.

THE PAT LINE

One of a number of escape networks across France, the Pat Line had been established by Pat O'Leary and was co-ordinated from Britain by 'the one-armed man' escapee from Dunkirk, Jimmy Langley.

From the summer of 1940, service men were returning from behind the lines with important information. Early returners were directed on arrival to Room 424 in the Metropole Hotel. Later, the increasing numbers of escapees were directed to the 'London Transit Camp', formerly the Great Central Hotel, opposite Marylebone Station. They climbed the staircase to opulent bedrooms now devoid of everything but a table and two chairs, to be questioned about their experiences on the run. Churchill demanded that all escapees be returned to their families within forty-eight hours of arrival, for humanitarian reasons, so the debriefing was swift and to the point.

The War Office had had an office dealing with prisoner-of-war camps during the First World War, but this office, headed by Norman Crockett, would have to deal with a quite different set of circumstances. This new section, called MI9, would be training servicemen who found themselves stranded in Europe to evade capture altogether. The intelligence they brought back with them was invaluable, though it encroached on the British Intelligence Services who were concerned that the returning evaders might undermine the secrecy of their agents out there in the field.

But a downed airman who returned was a boost to morale. Moreover, a pilot could take two years to train, so getting each one back was a bonus – good reasons for this underfunded little outfit to exist. But underfunded it remained.

In January 1942, in a room in eastern Germany, Lieutenant Airey Neave put on his imitation German military overcoat, his cardboard leggings blackened to look like jackboots, his cardboard belt and holster, and his cap badge with the swastika carved from old linoleum. Alongside a Dutchman similarly attired, he walked out on to the terrace into the snow, down a spiral staircase, past the guardroom, and into the courtyard. The German sentries saluted as the two 'officers' went for a stroll into town. Neave had just escaped the highest security German prisoner-of-war camp, Colditz.

It was still a long way to Britain. Smuggled out of Switzerland and through France, he was astonished at the efficiency of the sequence of helpers, passing him between safe houses like an express parcel – this was the genius network run by Pat O'Leary – and on to a very well-paid guide who took the group on a dangerous and weatherbeaten journey across the Pyrénées. A moment of terror ensued at the southern Spanish border – fugitives caught in Spain would be interned in atrocious conditions at the Spanish concentration camp

Miranda de Ebro south of Bilbao – but Neave was lucky and made it into Gibraltar. From there he was whisked away for questioning at the Great Central Hotel – the 'London Transit Camp'.

In the hotel bar, he ran into an old friend, now with only one arm. They'd last seen each other side by side on stretchers in a hospital in France, both wounded and stranded at Dunkirk. Despite his disability, or perhaps because of it, Jimmy Langley had escaped via Marseilles, a French prison and a medical repatriation. Meanwhile, Airey Neave had been sent to the horrors of Stalag XXA in Poland where he escaped, got caught and ended up with the other 'difficult' prisoners in Colditz. Neave was not the first to escape from Colditz but he was the first to make it all the way back home – the first 'home run' and a testament to Pat O'Leary and his compatriots.

The meeting with Langley in the hotel bar was no accident – over lunch, Neave was asked to join MI9. Langley and Neave became the only co-ordinators for the networks helping Allied servicemen to escape: their only source of funds, equipment, information. Two men, one room, a few filing cabinets. As Neave said, 'In the world of military intelligence, we were extremely small beer'.

But MI9 agents in France were resourceful. When Belgian doctor Albert-Marie Guérisse found himself stranded in France and under arrest, he announced to the police officer that he was an evading Canadian airman called Patrick Albert O'Leary. If they'd discovered he was an SOE agent, he'd have been shot. Instead, as a prisoner of war, he was sent to the internment camp near Nîmes where he orchestrated his escape with the co-operation of every other prisoner in the camp. En masse they mounted a mock jailbreak, keeping the French guards occupied while O'Leary climbed out the back through a cell window. The flat above a doctor's surgery in Marseilles proved a safe hiding spot. And Langley was keen to keep him there.

Pat O'Leary was the epitome of the resourceful adventurer, a leader liked by everyone who worked with him. In a year, the Pat Line rescued 600, moving them safely to Gibraltar and from there to Britain. Not long after that, however, fifty of those on the Pat Line would be in prison, betrayed by a traitor amongst them. Pat O'Leary found himself at Natzweiler-Struthof concentration camp in Alsace, with fellow inmate Brian Stonehouse, a wireless operator code-named Celestin. Torquay-born Brian Stonehouse would become a famous painter and fashion artist after the war. During their time at the camp, Stonehouse painted many famous portraits of the inmates and guards, including one of Pat O'Leary.

The 'Pat Line' delivered Dumais and many others to the 'beach house' at Canet-Plage but this was no seaside holiday. Every available space in the little cottage was crowded with escaping airmen and evaders from across occupied France – sixty-five of them spent three horrific days and nights waiting for the first attempt to collect them by boat. No luck. After three hours of shivering on the beach, the boat had not arrived and they were herded back into the cottage, disappointed. And no luck the second night either. Just one more attempt and the mission would be cancelled.

On the third night, the escapees spread out along the beach, eyes straining for a glimpse of any dark shape on the water and, to their relief, the boats appeared, but they were no bigger than dinghies meant to hold two people and the oarsmen. Nevertheless, eight men were carried by each dinghy, dangerously low in the water, in each journey out to the carrier. Out on the water, Dumais expected to see at least a small destroyer to take the sixty-five of them, but the smell told him otherwise – this was just a fishing trawler. And for the next week they would be sleeping out on the open deck, on the long journey south to Gibraltar, not even with room for them all to lie down at the same time.

The fishing trawler was run by Poles on behalf of the Royal Navy. Unfortunately, with the delays, the ship was already running out of food and fresh water. Within a few days they were down to half a cup of water and a biscuit per day for each man and they were expected to work, repainting the ship to camouflage it from any German patrols. Whenever a plane flew overhead, the fugitives had to make themselves scarce; hiding below decks, crammed under nets or dinghies. The minute there was a breeze, the sails went up to save on fuel and the ship maintained the constant appearance of a working fishing boat travelling at a maximum speed of just 6 knots. Constantly hungry, thirsty and scared, it was a slow journey through hell – well, perhaps not quite hell, but certainly purgatory.

On the fifth night, at 3 a.m., they were awoken by two loud explosions and a voice bellowing in English, 'What ship are you?' The identifying reply from the captain astonished Dumais. Apparently for all this time they'd been travelling on the Royal Navy's HMS *Sea Lion*!

At Gibraltar German spies were everywhere and the ship had to maintain her disguise. Even here the fugitives had to hide. As the ship docked, the longshoremen fashioned a corridor out of packing cases from the ship to a nearby warehouse so the escaping soldiers and airmen could make it to the shore undetected.

Though still in hiding, Dumais was on British soil and at least he had options now. He could get to Plymouth by seaplane or submarine, by motor boat to Dartmouth or Falmouth, or even travel by navy ship. Each option took him across the enemy-infested waters of the English Channel, but eventually, after months of desperation and luck, he would make it back to England alive.

When Lucien Dumais reached the 'London Transit Office' of MI9, the one-armed man asked him if Dumais would consider setting up an operation like that of Pat O'Leary and the HMS *Sea Lion*. Not surprisingly, Dumais' instant response was a most definite 'No'. He'd had his fill behind enemy lines. Jimmy Langley smiled. He understood. And asked Dumais to contact him again if he ever changed his mind. 'Never,' was Dumais' last thought on the matter.

'Never' didn't last very long – Dumais would be going back sooner than he thought.

KADULSKI'S FELUCCAS

As Poland fell to the Nazis, Polish servicemen fled to France only to be trapped again when France succumbed. But as 1940 proceeded into 1941, strained British resources still couldn't help them. So Lieutenant Marian Kadulski, head of the Polish Naval Mission at Gibraltar, found himself an ancient 10-ton felucca called *Dogfish* and, in darkness, transported Polish men off the French beaches. As first lieutenant of the Polish Navy ship *Blyskawica*, he'd served in the Norwegian campaign and was a skilled sailor.

Conditions aboard *Dogfish* were primitive, with little shelter from the appalling weather. The engine often failed, so under sail the journeys could take over two weeks, even when he upgraded the service to the two 20-ton feluccas *Seawolf* and *Seadog*, which would transfer the fugitives to a 200-ton trawler at sea, eventually reaching Plymouth via Gibraltar.

Calling himself Krajewski for these clandestine missions, he rescued hundreds of Polish escapees during 1941 and 1942 and landed a few Polish agents in France, showing the British what could be achieved in fishing boats under the noses of the Germans. Polish fishing boat HMS *Sea Lion* continued his fine example.

Most of the Polish escapees rescued by Kadulski would join the Polish Navy in exile in Britain, reporting to the Polish Navy Southern Command headquarters in Albert Rd, Devonport.

THE COMET LINE

In August 1941, four strangers turned up at the British consulate in Bilbao, Spain. One of them was an evading soldier who spoke no French, two were Belgian Officers eager to join the Allies, the fourth was a frail girl, Andrée de Jongh, daughter of a Brussels schoolmaster, and she had an amazing story to tell. Andrée had established a series of safe houses from Belgium to the Pyrénées and wanted help from the British to move hundreds of evaders back to Britain via Gibraltar.

Andrée was tougher than she appeared, guiding the aircrew over the rugged tracks through the Pyrénées in all weather. To begin with the head of MI6 didn't trust a woman to do the job (strange considering so many of the evaders owed their lives to the courage of women in France and Belgium). But when in 1942 Andrée delivered all seven of the crew of an RAF heavy bomber safely to Gibraltar and all within a week of them being shot down at the Dutch/Belgian border, even MI6 had to admit she was worthy of their attention. Her network became the Comet Line, and she and her team rescued fifty-four evaders in just four months, all coming through the ports and airfields of south-west England to freedom.

One of the Comet Line guides was Albert Johnson, an Englishman who had been working in Brussels before the war, and found himself stranded on the border between France and Spain. And there he remained, code-named 'B', guiding 122 fugitives across the Pyrénées to freedom. He was fortunate to escape arrest by the Germans, and after the war, Albert Johnson lived and married in Devon, bringing up three children. Another Comet Line guide who survived, Peggy van Lier, would eventually be smuggled into Britain via Gibraltar, and would marry Jimmy Langley in 1944.

There would be many other escape networks across France and Spain, mostly heading for Gibraltar, but Germans spies were infiltrating the teams and one by one, the members were arrested and networks disabled. Escape through Spain soon became impossible and, by 1943, MI9 was anxious to find a reliable alternative route via the western beaches of France. The Motor Gun Boats at Dartmouth geared themselves up for sea rescues across the Channel but they still needed the right agent to go into France and establish a new route to the sea, and that agent would be Lucien Dumais.

GETTING
HOME

Janine Jouanjean didn't think much of this RAF pilot. Well, not at first. Her brother Georges had joined the French Resistance and was regularly bringing home Allied airmen on the run and she was always eager to help. She hated the Germans, even more since November 1942 when they'd broken the armistice deal and invaded Vichy France.

So Janine joined her brother and the latest airman riding their bicycles to the next safe house, her married sister's house. It was always good to have a girl along for these journeys. The 'puppet' Vichy Government had just decreed that all Frenchmen over 20 had to report for compulsory factory work in Germany – the Germans were definitely in charge now – and two young men going somewhere on bicycles might attract the soldiers' attention. Out cycling with pretty Janine, on the other hand, well, she would provide a distraction.

Riding along the narrow lanes, Janine glanced at their fugitive. His clothes were very shabby and he was a year younger than her, about 19, but he was quite good looking – for an Englishman.

In fact the airman Gordon Carter had been born and grown up in Paris. His English parents then moved to the United States and, when war broke out, he crossed the border to Canada to join up. Captivated by the air force and demonstrating a maturity and intelligence beyond his youth, he soon became a pilot and in 1942, he was assigned to the Pathfinders, an elite force established to lead the bombers to their targets. On 13 February 1943, he was on his

fourteenth mission – leading the bombers to the German submarine pens at Lorient – when heavy flak took out his Halifax's engine.
Carter and his crew baled out.

As Carter parachuted down a French lad literally caught him,
declaring 'Tu es mon frère' (You are my brother). Carter was lucky;
his French was excellent and he'd already spent most of his life in
France. The Halifax's gunner landed nearby and there was no sign of
the rest of the crew, so Carter and the gunner started walking for the
south east, thinking their best course was to try for Spain.

They briefly stayed with a French family, wisely pretending to
be Canadian airmen. As it turned out this family weren't too fond
of the British, particularly after the bombing of the French navy at
Mel-el-Kébir. Even after two years, some of the French were still
holding grudges.

The pair met with a local Resistance leader who arranged for a
pickup by submarine from the northern coast of the Brittany peninsula. It took some getting there, avoiding German sentries and
French police, but eventually they were crouching in the darkness
behind rocks on the shore waiting for a signal from the submarine.
One signal flash and then nothing ... No pickup.

For the next week they were sheltered in a Cistercian monastery,
before being collected by Georges Jouanjean, a newly recruited

Brittany would see the collection of a number of soldiers, refugees and secret
agents. Some pickups were successful; some were not. (Library of Congress,
LC-USZ62-91349)

guide for the Pat Line. Georges intended to take them to Paris since the way south was now blocked. However, Pat O'Leary had been captured along with many of the helpers and Georges quickly discovered that the safe house in Paris had its cover blown too. As he approached the safe house, there were Gestapo officers at the door and Georges was soon running for his life down the stairs, along the street, German guns blazing.

So it was back to Brittany, for a cycle ride with Janine to her married sister's house. All escape routes were down; he would just have to lay low for a while. And that meant a fortnight with Janine, going to the cinema, long walks in the country, cycle rides. While the Resistance were desperately finding a way to get Carter back home, he and Janine were falling in love.

One day Georges appeared with a plan to steal a German Motor Torpedo Boat (MTB) and drive Gordon Carter back to England. Perhaps he wasn't happy about Carter dating his sister, but it still seemed a very risky idea. Gordon was willing to give it a go, hoping Janine would come with him – though that was of course impossible, even he could see that. It was too dangerous for Janine but Gordon's continuing presence was increasingly dangerous for her and her family. Gordon Carter had to go home.

Saying goodbye was hard, and they made no promises, but Carter told himself he would come back to France to be with Janine.

The plan involving a German MTB was soon abandoned. Now at Tréboul, Carter joined a group of eighteen Frenchmen trying to get to England to join the war, travelling on a 40-foot sardine pinnace the *Dalc'h-Mad*, skippered by Louis Marec. The Germans now controlled every port and there were German sentries patrolling the quay at Tréboul. The pinnace was in the mud of low tide and, under cover of darkness, the men filed down the hill towards her, then huddled waiting for the right moment. Each time the sentries turned their backs, one man from the group sprinted from the darkness, jumped down into the mud and clambered up on to the *Dalc'h-Mad*.

The escapees filled the ship's tiny hold, cramped below deck and unable to move, huddled in absolute silence as the sentries continued pacing the quayside. It seemed hours before daybreak when the tide would rise and the ship float up off the mud. And then Louis Marec and his two-man crew boarded the boat and readied her for the voyage.

Brittany coastline. (Author's collection)

At the harbour entrance, boats had to stop for a final check at the German guardhouse. Sometimes the sentries boarded the boats for an inspection. The *Dalc'h-Mad*'s captain idled the boat alongside the harbour wall, but left a big enough gap to dissuade anyone thinking of boarding. Meanwhile the men in the hold held their breaths.

At the same moment, two members of the Resistance arrived at the guardhouse. The first claimed to be a workman ordered to do some urgent and very disruptive repairs. The second man complained loudly that someone had scraped his car – was it the workman? A furious argument broke out in the guardhouse. The distracted German sentries waved the *Dalc'h-Mad* on her way. Nineteen men in the hold let out a collective sigh of relief.

The boat chugged out across the Bay of Biscay, past the German destroyers at Brest, past the German patrolling zones and out across the English Channel. As night fell, the boat rocked violently in force 9 gales, the seasick passengers desperately holding on as the hold filled up with salt water, diesel and their own vomit. Gordon Carter must have wished he'd stayed with Janine. Fortunately the storm had probably grounded any German aircraft sent out to find them when they hadn't returned to Tréboul on time.

The storm abated and finally they felt safe. As Gordon Carter describes:

Lizard Point. (Library of Congress, LC-DIG-ppmsc-08225)

We ran up a French tricolour with a cross of Lorraine, the emblem of the Free French, on it. We had water to drink but no food. After a fine day riding the swell, without as much as sighting a ship or plane, we sprang a leak which no amount of bailing could contain. The seamen among us managed to stretch a large piece of sail under the hull, and we were thus able to continue on our way. That night we ran into a thick fog bank. When dawn broke, our third day out of Tréboul, we sighted a coastline on the horizon ahead of us. As we slowly put-putted towards it, a small fishing craft approached. English? Irish? French? We stood off, waiting either to welcome it or fight. It turned out to be a Cornish crabber. It guided us through a minefield (we hadn't even thought of that hazard!) to the lifeboat slipway on Lizard Point. We made fast alongside the ramp and I told the bobby and the few locals who had gathered who we were. Tea and sandwiches were brought and then we were escorted by two naval vessels to Newlyn. I was incredibly relieved to be home and very happy to be safe again.

But from the moment Gordon Carter landed in Cornwall, his thoughts were of Janine. She and her family had risked so much to help him and now he had left them to an uncertain future. Anonymous tip-offs reached the German authorities every day and thousands of French citizens were sent to concentration camps for aiding the Allies.

Two months after Gordon's escape, Georges Jouanjean and his mother were betrayed and arrested by the Nazis. In a prison in Rennes, Georges was forced to watch his mother being beaten. He too was beaten and tortured in a cold-water bath before being locked up in a cage barely 4-foot square; slumped inside like a trapped animal, he couldn't sit, stand or lie down. He expected to be shot any day but what happened to him was worse – a tour of concentration camps. First Birkenau, where he was tattooed before the German bureaucrats realised there was a mistake – Georges wasn't Jewish, so he was in the wrong place. So on to Buchenwald, then Flossenbürg where typhus was rife. If there was a hell in hell, he'd found it.

Gordon Carter lay in his bunk worried he would never see Janine again. His return had boosted morale among the Pathfinders – he was a hero – but he thought only of Janine and pencilled her name above his bunk. He wrote letters to her that he couldn't send and, when he went back on operations, the 1,000-pound bomb loaded on his plane for the next raid had 'Pour Janine' painted on it.

Langley at MI9 took a great interest in Gordon Carter's escape – would Gordon like to help them re-establish the 'Pat Line'? But Gordon said 'No', knowing that his reappearance in France might endanger Janine. After just two weeks' sick leave to 'calm his nerves', Gordon Carter was back with the Pathfinders, flying over France.

Even after D-Day, June 1944, as Brittany was liberated by the Allied Forces, Janine Jouanjean didn't know if she would ever see Gordon Carter again. She knew he'd arrived safely in England back in 1943 – an agreed cryptic message on the BBC radio service had told her he was home. But she'd not heard a word since. She'd lost her brother and mother, and now amongst all the dancing, cheering crowds watching the liberating tanks and trucks driving through, Janine was feeling incredibly alone.

One day in August 1944, a huge bundle of letters arrived at Janine's door. The post had been restored between Britain and France and all of Gordon's letters arrived at once. She read them in one sitting, thrilled at last that there was hope they would see each other again. He'd missed her as much as she had missed him. It was a wonderful moment.

And then another letter arrived, from Gordon's aunt. Gordon had been shot down again and was now a prisoner of war in Germany.

BONAPARTE
BEACH

When Jimmy Langley asked Lucien Dumais to return to occupied France to establish a new escape route by sea, Dumais' first response had been a definite 'No'.

Escape lines for downed airmen and other fugitives through Spain and Gibraltar had been compromised, but the 15th Motor Gun Boat Flotilla at Dartmouth (*see* Chapter 10) were already gearing up for a new escape route by sea. They just needed the right agent to get the 'parcels' across France to Plouha on the Brittany coast. Pickup from the isolated little beach at Plouha seemed the best option, at a time when the Germans were heavily fortifying French shores.

But Lucien Dumais' refusal was adamant – he was never going to go back there again. Back in England, Dumais had faced interrogation by all the top brass. He had made it through France mostly without help and the senior officers, including Lord Louis Mountbatten and Douglas Fairbanks Jnr, were eager to hear every detail. But still Dumais refused to return to France – he'd been lucky to survive Dieppe. Something, however, was going to happen to change his mind.

By mid-1943, North Africa was back in the hands of the Allies and their armies were about to cross the Mediterranean, advancing into mainland Europe. Dumais went back with his battalion in Tunisia, eager for the fight to come, until the new platoon commander arrived …

Fresh from Canada, the new commander 'knew it all', frustratingly unaware of his own ignorance, putting on airs that profoundly annoyed an experienced fighter like Lucien Dumais. Perhaps the flaw lay with Dumais, his fierce personality unsuited to taking orders, but it seemed to Dumais that the man in charge didn't know what the hell he was talking about.

And so Dumais was soon back in London, sitting on a park bench with Jimmy Langley in St James' Park, a chill in the air as Langley described the dangers of returning to France. If the Gestapo caught Dumais, MI9 couldn't help him. 'As far as we are concerned,' said the one-armed man, 'you will have ceased to exist.'

Langley had secret reservations about Lucien Dumais. He saw Dumais as a hot-head, perhaps unsuited to the mission after all and he set about testing the man. Langley had spies follow Dumais, checking on his girlfriends, getting him drunk in pubs and asking questions, even having him picked up by the police on trumped-up charges to see how Dumais would react. Dumais got angry, fed up of always being on his guard. When a captain from the Free French Forces rudely demanded to know why Dumais was wearing a medal he wasn't entitled to, Dumais lost his temper, his seething response in vitriolic French. The French captain grinned; he was just testing Dumais' accent and was satisfied. Dumais' Canadian French could pass for central France, so they constructed a background for him accordingly. From now on, he would be Lucien Desbiens, a funeral director. 'Glad to have you with us,' Langley informed Dumais and that was it.

Lucien Dumais was soon on his way back to France along with wireless operator Raymond Le Bosse, another French-speaking Canadian with experience of escaping from France. Their first flights were nearly shot out of the air, but at last Lucien and Ray were on the ground, in the hands of a very efficient reception committee. The situation in Paris, however, was desperate. The agents met with Christine and Suzanne who were running a hairdresser's that was the headquarters for an escape route for downed airmen, sending their 'parcels' south across Spain, but Christine was already in debt for 40,000 francs trying to keep the feeble escape lines open and the airmen were just ending up in Spanish gaols. On their next attempt to get the fugitives to the railway station, Christine and Suzanne were arrested. Suddenly Dumais and his wireless operator were completely on their own.

But not for too long. There were old contacts still around, some of whom had been in hiding for six months. Meeting quietly in a series of cafés and hotel rooms, Dumais managed to recruit a series of contacts from Paris to Brittany and eventually Dumais was introduced to François Le Cornec, head of a Resistance group who ran a café and charcuterie in Plouha. Le Cornec was the ideal man to take charge of the beach during the missions which were code-named BONAPARTE.

However, the beach was not the ideal location the British believed. The shingle and sandy shore were fine, but behind it was a sheer cliff, 100-feet high. To the south was another small cove with a road leading to a quay, which might have been better, but the quay had been deliberately blocked by submerged rocks – the Germans were making sure any enemy boats approaching at night would be wrecked.

Le Cornec was going to have to get his 'parcels' down the sheer cliff instead, though on second inspection there was enough of an incline to prevent the men falling to their deaths. It was a 100-foot drop sliding down on your backside to get to the beach. He hoped his fugitives would all be healthy and desperate enough to attempt it. At least the Germans weren't expecting that.

Eventually the network was established. The airmen and agents would get a train from Paris, pretending to be exhausted workers and falling asleep on the train to dissuade any dangerous conversation. The train would get them to a safe house at Saint-Brieuc on the north Brittany coast, where guides would take them in small numbers to Plouha to hide in nearby farmhouses. Dumais' wireless operator contacted London – the first pickup was on for 15 December 1943.

And then it wasn't. The winter gales delayed the operation for another month, leaving Dumais and his wireless operator living in a cold and flea-infested room above Le Cornec's café. Meanwhile, more and more airmen were coming into Paris. At last the secret message was relayed to them via the BBC radio broadcasts: 'Bonjour, tout le monde à la maison d'Alphonse' – Hello to everyone at Alphonse's house. The first mission was go.

On the evening of 28 January 1944, seventeen airmen were brought together for the first time along with six French Resistance guides and Le Cornec for a final briefing by Dumais. At midnight, a strange single-file of people approached the cliff through the inky darkness, each hanging on to the coat-tail of the one in front, and Marie-Thérèse, the only woman, leading the line. At the cliff-edge, they could see the waves a very long way down. Dumais was one of the last to slide down the hillside and he could feel himself almost rolling head first. Thankfully no one was hurt.

On either side, just 500 yards each way, were German listening posts but the darkness, the cliff and the roar of the sea would mask their escape. As Dumais reached the beach, Marie-Thérèse was already signalling at sea level and at 1.15 a.m., three dark shapes approached the beach. It took them just twelve minutes to get the seventeen passengers into the small boats and on their way to the Motor Gun Boat anchored off shore, Dumais and his French colleagues shivering in the bitterly cold water. Dumais would not forget that freezing water for the rest of his life.

Meanwhile, Airey Neave was anxiously pacing up and down in the tiny MI9 office in London, waiting for news. By dawn, the fugitives were safely crossing the Channel on their way to Dartmouth.

And so the Shelburne Line was established, nicknamed the 'boat train', such was its success. It was hard work with many tense moments – the Germans firebombed one house suspected of hiding the escaping airmen, but fortunately no one was hurt. Dumais kept the line running for five more months, bringing 307 airmen back to England in time for D-Day.

KILLING
'PIMPERNEL SMITH'

As Europe fell to the Nazis, there was still a need for commercial flights from Britain into Europe, but of course, these were now very dangerous endeavours. Dutch pilots for KLM airlines operated one of the two remaining civilian services, from Whitchurch Airport near Bristol, flying the precarious route across the Channel from south-west England to Lisbon Airport in neutral Portugal.

This civilian route was officially protected from German attacks, though the British regularly used these planes to ferry spies via south-west England in and out of occupied Europe, despite the German officials in Lisbon checking every passenger list.

At 9.30 a.m. on 1 June 1943, the passengers at Lisbon Airport boarded one of these flights, Flight 777 – a Douglas DC-3 – heading for south-west England. Among them were: Gordon MacLean, inspector general of His Majesty's Consulates; Tyrell Shervington, general manager of Shell in Portugal, though the Germans suspected that he was a British spy; Ivan Sharp, who was an industrial spy investigating German steel supplies; and Wilfrid Israel, a Jewish businessman who had rescued hundreds of Jews from the Nazis just before the war, and who had been in Spain negotiating an escape route for Jewish refugees. Also on board was the Hollywood star Leslie Howard, returning to Britain after a strangely timed European lecture tour on acting and *Hamlet*.

At 11 a.m., the Dutch captain of Flight 777, Quirinius Tepas, informed his superiors that they were under attack. That was the last anyone heard from the aircraft as it plunged into the Bay of Biscay, taking with it the lives of everyone onboard: four Dutch crewmen and thirteen passengers, including Leslie Howard.

Flight 777 was the only plane lost in this civilian route during the Second World War; the only flight targeted by the Germans. Why did the Germans shoot down this particular civilian plane? Of course, some of the passengers were probably spies, but they had travelled many times on the civilian service. Why choose that plane and not others? Many believe the Germans were targeting Leslie Howard because of a film he made in 1942 called *Pimpernel Smith*, which had become very popular in America and occupied Europe, primarily because of the film's audacious final line:

> Don't worry, I'll be back. We will all be back.

This final line of *Pimpernel Smith* was a beacon of hope for European audiences struggling under occupation. Certainly Goebbels, the German Minister for Propaganda, was furious, as the titular hero played by Leslie Howard rescued political prisoners and refugees under the very nose of the Nazis and more than hinted that Germany was going to lose the war. Lord Haw Haw announced that when the Germans landed in Britain, they would 'get Leslie Howard'.

Howard was one of Britain's greatest actors and a Hollywood movie star, probably most famous now for playing Ashley Wilkes in *Gone With the Wind*. So was it just a strange coincidence that, on 1 June 1943, Göring's air force shot down Flight 777? It was part of a 'protected' service, one of only two civilian air companies permitted to fly between occupied Europe and Britain and the only plane on that service ever to be shot out of the sky.

Howard was of Polish descent and had served during the First World War, suffering from shell shock after his experiences as a soldier. He was incensed at the treatment of his countrymen when the Second World War saw Hitler invade Poland, and he left Hollywood in 1940 with the deliberate intention of making a film in Britain that would upset the Nazis and encourage the Resistance. Working with a Russian writer, Anatole de Grunwald, Howard produced and directed *Pimpernel Smith* in 1941, under the auspices of the Anglo-American Film Corporation. It was a film not only aimed at occupied European audiences but also designed to encourage the Americans to join the war effort.

Although a little dated now, it's an incredible achievement – propaganda disguised as light comedy – and it's worth taking a moment to consider *Pimpernel Smith* in more detail.

The film is set in Spring 1939, before Britain's declaration of war, with Howard's archaeologist wandering around Germany pretending to be a vague and forgetful academic while secretly rescuing political refugees from the Nazi regime, including prisoners from concentration camps. The story is very reminiscent of Baroness Orczy's famous novel *The Scarlet Pimpernel* set in Revolutionary France, hence the title.

The film's early location in the German Ministry of Propaganda is a blatant attack on Goebbels, where the film depicts a Nazi officer declaring straight to the camera: 'In Nazi Germany no one can be hoped to be saved by anybody.' The fictional German commander von Graum, portrayed in the film by British actor Francis L. Sullivan, is depicted as an obese idiot, repeatedly foiled by British intelligence and cunning – he's a double for Hermann Göring, head of the Luftwaffe. Did an angry Göring deliberately order Howard's plane to be shot down for this insult?

Civilisation itself is being destroyed by the Nazis, according to Howard's use of imagery in the film. In Britain, Howard's character admires the face and form of a classical Greek statue 'Aphrodite Goddess of Love', while in Berlin, General von Graum has similar classic paintings adorning his walls, but the shots show only the buttocks of the nudes behind the commander – in Howard's eyes, the German officers are just a 'series of arses'.

While the disguised hero and chief villain are bickering about whether Shakespeare was German, the realistic situations for Smith's escaping refugees are telling – Howard and his writer based these events on true stories. If audiences still considered the film to be merely light entertainment, Pimpernel Smith's final words to the German general were certainly sufficient to anger the German authorities:

> You will never rule the world because you are doomed. All of you who have demonised and corrupted a nation are doomed. Tonight you will take the first step along a dark road from which there is no turning back … there will be no dawn until at last you are lost and destroyed. You are doomed, Captain of Murderers, and one day sooner or later you will remember my words.

In *Pimpernel Smith*, Howard created an archetype of resistance, defeating the German military forces with cleverness and wit. But Howard wasn't killed just because of a film.

Leslie Howard was also a spy.

WITH FRIENDS LIKE THESE

Just before she died, the actress Conchita Montenegro gave a rare interview declaring that her ex-lover Leslie Howard had been tasked by British Intelligence to keep General Franco's Spain out of the war.

As the war escalated, Spain had declared herself neutral, officially refusing to take sides. After a brutal civil war, Spain's government did not really have the resources to fight again and Spanish dictator Franco received a great deal of money from the British to keep Spain neutral. But Spain was full of Nazi sympathisers and German spies and unofficially thousands of Franco's forces, known as the Blue Division, joined with Germany on the Eastern Front to fight against the Communists.

In 1943, the Allies knew that if they were to have any hope of successfully landing an invading force on the western European mainland, they needed to keep Hitler busy on the Eastern Front. Getting Franco to withdraw his troops serving with the Germans would make a big impact, but how to convince Franco without destroying his official neutrality?

The Spanish film star Conchita Montenegro became Leslie Howard's lover in 1931 when they were both in Hollywood. Howard would have a string of lovers during his career and he remained friends with all of them. Meanwhile, Montenegro returned to Spain and in 1943 she was romantically linked with the Spanish diplomat Ricardo Giménez Arnau, a senior member of the far right Falangist party. They married in 1944.

In that fateful spring of 1943, Leslie Howard was on a lecture tour of Spain and Portugal, giving talks on 'The Actor's Approach to *Hamlet*'. Strange timing for acting lessons, and Howard was reported to be unusually nervous about the tour.

Conchita Montenegro later declared that Leslie Howard had met secretly with Winston Churchill before the European tour and had been given instructions to do what he could to keep Spain out of the war and convince General Franco to withdraw his unofficial troops.

She described how she and Howard met again while he was touring in Spain and, using her contacts, she arranged a meeting between Howard and General Franco.

On Tuesday, 1 June 1943, Flight 777 set out from Lisbon Airport at 9.30 a.m. It was a Douglas DC-3, a reliable aircraft with many hours in the air and a very experienced Dutch crew. As usual, the German Forces reported the aircraft was in flight and expected to be told, as usual, to let the civilian service continue on its way. However, on that day they reported Flight 777 was in the air and received the order 'Shoot it down'. Even the German airmen were surprised, but they obeyed and Flight 777 plunged into the Bay of Biscay.

In October 1943, General Franco ordered the Blue Division to return to Spain. Most of his forces complied with the order and they left behind a German army who would have to fight the Russians with significantly reduced numbers. So was Leslie Howard instrumental in keeping Spain neutral in the war and encouraging Franco to withdraw any support for the Nazis? There's nothing on record to offer an answer, only rumours and hearsay and the word of an ageing Spanish film star.

Was Leslie Howard a spy at all? Perhaps not, though evidence suggests he was doing something clandestine and, for a film-maker, he had some unusual friends. At the time of his death, Howard was living with his lover Josette Ronserail in a house in Slough. She was a courier for the Special Operations Executive, having been recruited from the Volontaires Français while she was working as a secretary in 1941. She left the SOE in 1943 because she was pregnant, though the name of the father is as much of a mystery as her actual duties for the SOE. She was certainly sent on at least one mission into occupied Europe; discovered amongst her possessions after she died was a signed photo of Leslie Howard with the message, 'You'd better come back soon, Josette!'

ANOTHER THEORY

The attack on Flight 777 raised a number of questions. Certainly it is known that there were other secret agents who regularly used the airline and who would also have warranted targeting – so why the focus on this particular flight? One theory involves Leslie Howard's associate on the tour – a man called Alfred Chenhalls – who bore a remarkable resemblance to Winston Churchill, even down to his love of big cigars. Churchill, at this time, was in Tunis and due to fly back to Britain, so it is possible that Chenhalls could have been mistaken for the British prime minister; definitely a valuable target for the Luftwaffe. However, the German spies in Lisbon had been following Chenhalls for weeks, accompanying Howard and frequenting the hotel and the restaurants. They would have known he wasn't Churchill, even from a distance crossing the tarmac to board the plane. Unless someone made a very stupid mistake …

BLACK SQUADRON

While these vital civilian aircraft were flying the 'protected' route from south-west England in and out of Lisbon, the south west was also actively engaged in espionage by air. Clandestine flights ran regularly from Devon and Cornwall into France, many involved in aerial reconnaissance, but other flights from Devon's Winkleigh Airfield were so secret that even the British military didn't know they existed.

On the night of Friday, 4 August 1944, two Lysander aircraft took off from an airfield in the middle of Devon on a very secret mission, heading for France. The airfield was RAF Winkleigh, constructed in 1940 on marshy moorland just north of Okehampton and was home to over 1,200 personnel.

As the two Lysanders entered French airspace, however, the British radar system picked up two unidentified aircraft and scrambled a Mosquito night fighter from the Royal Canadian Air Force at RAF Colerne in pursuit.

But these were no enemy planes. The Allies were mistakenly attacking their own aircraft. Both Lysanders were from RAF 161 'Black Squadron', their secret aircraft painted all black, and their mission (as part of ongoing operations for the SOE) was to ferry French secret agents back to France.

The first Lysander was piloted by Jack Alcock and his passenger was Lucien Germereau, alias Lucien Pradier of the Scarlet Network of the French Resistance, returning home after a secret debriefing in London. D-Day had come and gone, the Allies were slowly taking back Europe from the Nazis, but the fighting was still raging in France. Consequently, Germereau and his colleagues were still sabotaging Nazi transport and communication lines, still reporting back to London on progress, and still bringing back maps and vital information.

But the Mosquito closed in and was unable to identify the black Lysander – there were no national markings. Thinking it was a Luftwaffe Henschel Ns126, the Mosquito pilot fired two bursts of cannon into the Lysander's fuselage. Alcock's fuel tank exploded and he and Germereau were killed instantly as the flaming Lysander crashed into a field near Messac in Brittany. It was a tragic accident.

The second Lysander landed safely in France and returned to RAF Winkleigh having collected Claude Antoinette Thierry-Mieg, a 26-year-old female agent for the Gallia network who had been working for the Resistance since November 1942. Her photo and details can be found here: www.cnd-castille.org/annuaire/item/2631-thierry-miegclaudeantoinette.html. Also with her was Leon Dupont, though little more is known of this French agent. They arrived safely in Devon at 5.50 a.m. on 5 August 1944.

On the night of Alcock's and Germereaus' tragic deaths, a further three Lysanders of the Black Squadron secretly left RAF Winkleigh for successful espionage missions into France.

David Freeman has written extensively about RAF Winkleigh, alongside his TV Series Secret Britain. *His excellent website can be found here:* http://jackiefreemanphotography.com/raf_winkleigh.htm.

GUNNER RÉE

Harry Rée was fed up. Having joined the army because his father was half-Jewish, he had been sent to Exeter to train as a gunner, pulling artillery on great wooden wheels. To Harry, it seemed like outdated nonsense – there was even talk of using horses. But even worse, the Exeter sergeant insisted on calling him Gonorrhoea instead of Gunner Rée. Everyone thought it was hilarious. But after six months of 'Come on Gonorrhoea!' Harry had had enough.

His brother had been a farmer in France and had barely escaped with the family to Britain when the Germans invaded in 1940. Now Harry's brother was working as an adviser to some people who were apparently being parachuted into France as secret agents. To Harry, that sounded much more exciting and – though his French wasn't good and it took four applications for him to gain approval – at last he was on his way to France in April 1943.

Harry requested that there be a reception committee when he landed by parachute – his French still wasn't that good, so he didn't want to mess things up in the first five minutes if he had to walk into a French village to ask for directions. But it was a disastrous landing – pitch dark and painful – and most of their gear landed in electric pylon wires. Fortunately they managed to find the wireless transmitter, otherwise bringing the operator René Maingard with him would have been a bit pointless.

But there was no one there to meet them.

Dogs started barking, so they made for the woods, like Boy Scouts traipsing through streams to try to lose the scent although their suitcases and heavy overcoats made them look exactly like the spies they were. They hid in the woods until dawn, only to be woken by another dog approaching. The dog's owner looked at the pair sleeping in the woods and declared, '*Je ne vous ai pas vu!*' – 'Haven't see you before!' This was the moment Harry had dreaded for months.

Harry said 'Bonjour' in his best French accent and the Frenchman smiled. The dog wagged its tail – it was a lovely mongrel. After a pause, the stranger asked them if they wanted any food – 'Like anything I would,' came Harry's reply, and the Frenchman fetched some ham, bread and wine from the farm where he worked. It wasn't quite the reception party they'd requested, but it was pretty good. They'd got lucky.

Actually, it was more than luck. The Nazis' invasion of Vichy France in November 1942 had backfired a little – the minute Frenchmen heard they were being conscripted into the German Army, many of them headed for the hills, literally, forming *Maquis* groups (bands of guerrilla fighters) actively disrupting, sabotaging and attacking German bases, factories and communication lines. The Nazis' oppression had vastly increased the French resistance and the supplies of arms, ammunition, explosives and trained agents from Britain were very welcome indeed. The dangers were still there – the repercussions on the French population were horrific – but the French were tired of the occupation, revolted by their Nazi oppressors and wanted to do something about it.

Harry and Maingard had been sent to assist Squadron Leader Maurice Southgate, survivor of the *Lancastria*, who was now head of one the largest Special Operations Executive circuits in France: the STATIONER circuit, organising sabotage missions and supplies and training for the Resistance. Harry was there to destroy the Michelin factory manufacturing tyres and caterpillar treads for the German Army.

But the Michelin job was cancelled and Harry was redirected to the hills in Jura near the Swiss border, where new Maquis groups were forming and in urgent need of wireless communications so they could order parachute drops of ammunition and supplies. Harry helped get them organised into a new circuit, STOCKBROKER, and soon there were hundreds of trained men and reception grounds for supply drops throughout the region. Arms and ammunition were then hidden in caves lined with vats of Beaujolais wine.

When Harry's first child arrived, he was still in France, living upstairs in a tumbledown cottage owned by a funny little 18-year-old man who'd left the priesthood. On 5 May 1943, they made their way to the ex-priest's parents' house who were not in the Resistance but who secretly listened to the BBC on the wireless – 'Clementine ressemble sa grand-mère' came the mysterious message from the BBC. No one else in France but Harry knew what it meant – his wife had given birth to a girl.

Taking some explosives out of the village in saddlebags on his bicycle one morning, he was stopped by the local *gendarmes* and asked for his ID. They asked him what was in the *les sacoches* – saddlebags. He replied it was just a few night things, but as he opened the *sacoches* with the explosives in the bottom, his leg started shaking. One of the *gendarmes* asked '*Vous avez froid?*' – Are you cold? 'Yes, it is a bit cold this morning, isn't it?' Harry replied in his politest French. The gendarme nodded and waved him on.

The members of the Maquis groups quickly became experts. Bothey, the baker at Dampierre, with his small team successfully sabo-taged railways in the frontier regions. Paupal, a draper from Chaussin, singlehandedly blew up a heavily laden troop train. However, it was a deadly game. One of the Maquis was captured – one of the Larsenieux brothers working with Harry – and the Germans retaliated against the 'terrorists', rounding up suspects in nearby Lons. Suddenly Harry Rée was on the run to Vallentigny near Montbéliard, to a hideout owned by the accountant at the local Peugeot factory.

A wrecked German tank. (Library of Congress, LC-USZ62-50118)

The Peugeot car works was now making turrets and engines for
German tanks and in the summer of 1943 the RAF bombers were
trying and failing to put the factory out of action. Also they risked
killing the French forced labourers. The factory had a complex,
unbreakable system of security passes so getting saboteurs into the
place was impossible. With the help of his accountant friend, Harry
Rée quietly went to see Rodolph Peugeot.

'Wouldn't it make more sense if we organised sabotage inside your
factory rather than having the RAF come again?' suggested Harry.

'Of course,' replied Monsieur Peugeot, and he offered Harry some
contacts inside the factory to make the appropriate arrangements.

'Please don't bomb the Peugeot factory anymore,' messaged Harry to
the RAF, but they took a little more convincing than Monsieur Peugeot.
Eventually the RAF agreed as long as Harry sent monthly reports.

Five Peugeot workers volunteered for the job. Their first task, they
decided, was to blow up the electricity supply. With pistols and plastic
blocks of explosives in their pockets, the workers made their way lei-
surely to the transformer house, stopping for a friendly game of football
with the German guards while a colleague unlocked the transformer
building. During the football game, a block of explosive fell out of a
worker's pocket. A German guard pointed at the plastic block and said in
a friendly manner, 'You've dropped something, sir, I think.' The worker
said, 'Merci', and calmly put the explosives back in his pocket.

Just after midnight on 6 November 1943, the transformer house
blew up. Next morning the workers stood around idly as the furious Gestapo investigated and arrested a few workers, but the culprits
escaped. The explosion had taken out the steel presses for the tank
turrets – there would be no more work for many weeks.

German engineers arranged for new presses to be sent from
Hanover, using barges along the Rhine-Doubs canal. This, however,
was just what Harry Rée and his friends had anticipated. The French
workers ambushed the first barge and, as the French barge crew ran
for their lives, explosives destroyed the barge, blocking the canal.

More steel presses arrived from Stuttgart on trucks under guard by
the SS. As the trucks reached the factory, they were ambushed, grenades and handmade bombs raining down from the roof of a building.

In the months that followed, the workers kept attaching plastic
explosive to machines and effectively stopped production – a fact clearly
demonstrated in the copy of Peugeot's monthly figures that Harry sent
to the RAF. Months after the first explosion, the Germans still couldn't

restart production and the factory produced nothing for the remainder of the war. Peugeot had successfully destroyed its own plant.

Harry Rée and his men went on to destroy thousands of gallons of oil at Usines Marti and badly damage the factory of the Leroy Machine Company at St Suz.

But the Gestapo were closing in on Harry. One of his team, Pierre Martin, turned out to be a double agent, endangering the whole network. Harry set a trap, waiting at a rendezvous with a pistol to kill Martin, but Martin had set a trap too, waiting at a café with disguised Gestapo agents. Suddenly men working for Rée were being caught and arrested. The Resistance insisted that Harry make for Switzerland. Harry hung on for as long as he could, but eventually he cycled to Hérimoncourt where a guide got him through the mountains to the Swiss border. He was interned in Switzerland but not for long.

Within four weeks he was back working in France. While Resistance fighters were being arrested, Rée was in hiding in Jura, always on the move, organising teams to assassinate Pierre Martin. But Martin was constantly surrounded by German guards. Many attempts to kill him failed, until one day there was an eyewitness report in a local paper, *Le Petit Comptoir*:

> Tuesday evening, at about 1950, guest dining in the restaurant of the Terrace Hotel in the rue Belfort, Besançon, were startled by the reverberations of a dozen revolver shots. Two young men who had been sitting at one of the tables, had fired the shots at another diner sitting alone, Monsieur P.M., who had just finished his meal and got up to leave the salon. Hit by several bullets in the chest, abdomen, and head, the victim expired within 20 minutes, although guests and the staff of the restaurant did everything to assist him. Taking advantage of the general confusion, the two assassins ran into the street and disappeared in the dark night. A German soldier chased them and fired. A woman, Madame Conraud, of Cite Rosemund, who happened to be passing by in the Avenue Carnot at the moment of the drama, was wounded in the leg by a stray bullet. She was taken to the Clinic Heitz in the rue de la Mouliere. The body of the victim was taken to the morgue of the Hospital Saint-Jaques …

The leader of Harry's assassination team was Jean Simon, a young bank clerk from St Claude. Simon continued as a successful saboteur, creating his own networks, but was killed by the Gestapo in another café gunfight in January 1944.

A café in France, perhaps not unlike the one where Pierre Martin waited with disguised Gestapo agents. (Author's collection)

Harry Rée was instructed by the British to quit the region but he refused. Instead, on Sunday, 27 November 1943, he went to see Jean Hauger, by day a schoolmaster and by night 'Macout', leader of the local Resistance. The schoolmaster's door was opened by a man in civilian clothes whom Harry had never seen before, pointing a pistol at him.

'Put your hands up,' said the man.

'Don't be an idiot,' said Harry. 'It's very dangerous to play with firearms like that. For Heaven's sake put it away.'

According to Harry, the man then pulled out his card which said 'Gestapo'. In fact he was a sergeant with the Geheime Feldpolizei.

'Oh, I beg your pardon,' said Harry, and put his hands up.

The officer ushered Harry inside and explained that Jean Hauger had been arrested (which wasn't true) and Hauger's old mother had been taken into custody. Harry declared he was just a teacher friend come to borrow a book. They sat waiting for the Security Service (the SD squad) to take Harry to Gestapo headquarters.

The officer reassured Harry that he would likely be cleared and that would be that. Harry knew better – to the Gestapo, Harry Rée was 'Henri', one of the most wanted men in France. He would never make it out of the Gestapo headquarters. His French was better, but would certainly break down under questioning.

'Are you a Gaullist?' the officer asked Harry.

'No,' Harry declared.

'Everyone's a Gaullist these days, aren't they?' the officer laughed.

'How about a drink?' Harry suggested.

'Do you know where the wine is?' the officer asked.

Harry nodded and found some glasses, then reached for the bottle in the cupboard behind the Gestapo official and brought the bottle crashing on the back of the officer's head.

Unfortunately Harry didn't hit him anything like hard enough. The officer turned and fired at point-blank range and, as he fired, Harry was hitting him and remembered thinking, 'Good heavens, how extraordinary – they must have blanks in there.' He didn't feel the impact of the bullets piercing his side.

It was a brutal fight. Harry tried to remember his training but could only remember *King Lear* – although his attempt to gouge out the officer's eye was in vain. Mère Hauger's dishes crashed to the floor and the officer hit Harry on the head with the pistol before pushing him down some stairs into a cellar. Harry managed to stand but the officer got him into a half-nelson hold and Harry struggled to breathe. But he was determined to survive to see his daughter. Harry hit the officer in the stomach, sending him crashing into a wall as he painfully cried 'Sortez, sortez' – go! Harry didn't wait for the translation.

Jean the schoolmaster had mentioned on a previous visit an escape route across the fields at the back, to the next village. Harry left his bike and his ID card still in the Gestapo's hands and ran for it. Through the pouring rain he stumbled and crawled through brambles into the woods; he was in danger of losing consciousness, but the fear of being caught kept him running. He could feel hot rain inside his jacket, put his hand in to find the leak and discovered blood – he was the one leaking. The officer hadn't been firing blanks after all.

Finally, Harry swam the river and made it to a little villa he knew from previous visits. A factory owner lived there who knew Harry, although he was horrified to discover a blood-spattered, bedraggled and soaked figure on his doorstep at 6 p.m. on a Sunday. '*Mon Dieu …*'

A doctor came – Harry had been shot three times, once through the chest, just above his heart, and two shots had pierced his lungs. They had to get him to a hospital in Switzerland urgently and that meant a terrible journey for the Resistance, getting a stricken Harry to the frontier where Harry gave himself up to the Swiss authorities. A British legation arranged for his recovery at Lake Lucerne.

Partly recovered, Harry was quickly back in France, making his way to the Pyrénées and heading for Britain. But the Spanish border

guards caught him and he was locked up in the notorious internment camp, Miranda de Ebro. It was July 1944 before he made it
back to Britain and he got to see his daughter for the first time.
She was 15 months old.

Harry had been in France a long time, facing danger and death
every day, all because he was fed up of the Exeter sergeant calling
him 'Gonorrhoea'.

And why did these agents do what they did? Was it patriotism?
Excitement? Perhaps the best explanation is in Harry Rée's own words:

> I can't say it was simple patriotism that moved most of us – there was
> very little of that in the last war, it was much closer to simple impatience.
> You see, after the fall of France most of us in the army in this country
> had damn all to do. We were pushed off to Exeter or Wales or Scotland,
> nice safe places where there was very little to do, while wives and fami-
> lies were often in London or Coventry or Plymouth, all places which
> were being bombed – they were at risk, while we weren't. I think a lot
> of men resented this. And there was another thing; if we were going
> to get into a risky situation, we wanted to go somewhere where we
> would be our own masters. We didn't want a stupid colonel ordering
> us to advance into a screen of machine-gun bullets when we didn't
> agree with the order – we weren't the Light Brigade. If we were going
> to advance into a screen of machine-gun fire or do something equally
> suicidal, we wanted it to be our own decision. That was something else
> we shared – and agreed about. But it made us all different. We were
> all individualists.

SPECIAL OPERATIONS PIGEONS

During the Second World War, a number of aircrew on operational
flights carried homing pigeons in case of emergencies and at RAF
Mount Batten there was a wartime pigeon loft with homing pigeons
trained to carry messages back to Plymouth. On 16 September 1944,
one pigeon arrived at Mount Batten carrying an SOS from a
Sunderland seaplane of No. 10 Squadron RAAF, the seaplane having
ditched into the sea.

Sometimes the pigeons would be dropped from an RAF plane over France so agents of the Special Operations Executive out in the field could send back messages. The received information could be very useful, though not if the Germans got hold of the pigeon first – then the message received was usually pretty rude.

The bird was parachuted down in a little cardboard cage with a bit of food and some water to keep it alive until the SOE agent retrieved it. Inside the cage would be a pencil and some rice paper so a note could be attached to the pigeon's leg for the return journey to Plymouth.

RAF Pilot Officer John Charrot remembers being concerned about the pigeon's welfare, making sure he found a nice quiet spot so the poor bird would land safely. Sadly though, food was pretty scarce for some SOE agents and RAF Squadron Leader Frank Griffiths soon got a little cynical about the pigeon landings: 'Some, I'm jolly certain, got eaten …'

THE SPY WHO
NEVER WAS

During 1944, the Allied Forces made preparations for the major offensive from south-west England across the English Channel and on to the beaches of Normandy. Originally planned for 5 June 1944, bad weather would delay them for twenty-four hours and so 6 June 1944 would famously become D-Day – the beginning of the end of the Second World War in Europe.

Across the West Country, village roads were overwhelmed with trucks and troop carriers. Tens of thousands of men from across the globe were camped out in fields, accommodated and trained in old forts like Crownhill Fort in Plymouth. Harbours were filled with invasion fleets, as far as the eye could see, and as the day approached the quaysides and slipways in every port along the south-west English coast became congested embarkation points.

As the south west became the most militarised zone in England, how did German intelligence not know about the invasion plans? Even as the ships left the English harbours for France, Hitler and his senior officers were convinced any Allied invasion would take place around Calais to the north, the narrowest part of the English Channel. But surely this military offensive from the West Country was too vast to miss?

During the preparations for D-Day, German Intelligence – the Abwehr – sent their agent 'Drake' on a secret reconnaissance mission into south-west England. Drake was a member of the Aryan World Order Movement, an extreme branch of Welsh nationalism, and he'd been recruited to become a spy for the Germans through a Welsh mercenary code-named 'Dagobert', who in turn had been recruited into this espionage ring by a Spanish Nazi-sympathiser the Germans called 'Arabel'.

Drake made his way to Taunton in 1944 and would have seen the increasing amount of military activity as he then made his way to Exeter. At Exeter he was stopped for having the wrong papers, but he was then released and allowed to travel further, before reporting back to his German contacts that there was no increased military activity in the West Country.

German Military Intelligence then reported to Hitler that the Führer was right, of course. The Allied invasion would come via Calais, just as Hitler predicted.

What Hitler didn't know was that Drake the Welsh spy in the West Country didn't exist. The Aryan World Order Movement didn't exist. The recruiter Dagobert didn't exist. They were all the invention of a Spanish chicken farmer called Juan Pujol García, who hated the Nazis so much that he offered to work as a secret agent for the Germans and everything he told them was completely made up.

Juan Pujol García was essentially one of life's failures. His father was a successful factory owner in Spain, but his own ventures never quite seemed to work out. He spent his national service in a cavalry regiment, disliking authority and hating horse riding, spending months with his 'buttocks on fire'. As the Spanish Civil War broke out in 1936,

García managed a chicken farm near Barcelona and was called up to serve in the Republican Army. He refused and was eventually discovered hiding out in a girlfriend's parents' house. He was imprisoned, expected to be shot, but managed to escape and before long he found work managing another poultry farm near the French border. But the local Republican councillors kept taking a huge cut of the profits and García found himself unable to do his job properly. With few other options, he volunteered for the Republican's Signal Corps, with a plan to desert as soon as

Portrait of Hitler. (Library of Congress, LC-USZ62-48839)

possible, only to find himself on the front line. From here, desertions to Franco's Nationalists were commonplace but dangerous – one deserter was executed in front of the entire battalion. Nevertheless, García made it successfully across the divide between the opposing trenches, only to find himself in a series of prison camps under Franco.

By the end of the Spanish Civil War, García had had his fill of bullies, and the Nazis were proving to be more of the same. As France succumbed to invasion and the British fought on, García knew he had to do something to help defeat the German Forces.

In January 1941, García's wife approached the British Embassy in Madrid saying she knew of a man willing to work as a spy in Germany or Italy. No one at the embassy was interested, so García tried an alternative way of applying for the job.

First, he became a spy for the Germans. He lied to his German contacts, declaring that he was being sent to work for the Spanish Embassy in London. The Germans were delighted. García was actually stuck in Lisbon, unable to get a visa to go to London, but he managed to send letters to his German contact as though he was already in London, saying that the letters were coming to them via a commercial pilot regularly flying between Lisbon in Portugal and Whitchurch Airport near Bristol (*see* Chapter 14). The Germans were fooled, and still delighted.

Every intelligence report García sent was complete fabrication. Sitting in Lisbon, he sent the kind of reports he thought a spy would send, creating munitions factories in Britain that didn't exist, training centres that had no basis in fact, vessels leaving harbours he'd never visited – being careful not to mention too many ships' names in case the Germans had already sunk them. His only sources of information were an old map of Britain, a tourist guidebook, newspapers coming into Lisbon, a dictionary, and a copy of *The British Fleet* in Portuguese. He declared that the train fare between Glasgow and London was just 87 shillings, and that there were military exercises on Lake Windermere. He even invented submerged troop carriers. And there was nothing they liked better in Glasgow, he said, than a 'litre of wine'. The Germans apparently believed every word.

His creative letters from Lisbon were only supposed to be a short-term solution while he made contact with the Allies and got himself to England. But further attempts to interest British Intelligence failed. They didn't trust him.

At the same time, British Intelligence had intercepted some disturbing messages from Madrid to Berlin professing to come from a German spy working in England called Arabel. But the information was so ludicrous, so bizarre, that they couldn't believe the agent was actually in England. (They were right.) Meanwhile, García's wife tried again to get the Allies' attention and in January 1942, she visited the United States Embassy in Lisbon where at last the Assistant Naval Attaché took her seriously.

It was then that García's work revealed its full potential. On 26 March 1942, he declared (falsely) to the Germans that the British were sending a large convoy from Liverpool to relieve the besieged island of Malta. Malta was in a desperate state, constantly under attack from German forces, but this was the first relief convoy sent from the United Kingdom – if it had existed. García's report was forwarded to Berlin and within days the German Navy fleet and the Luftwaffe were preparing to ambush this non-existent convoy. A lie from a Spanish chicken farmer was influencing the decisions in Berlin.

Suddenly MI5 in London became aware of Juan Pujol García – was it possible that this Spanish chicken farmer was the agent Arabel, pretending to be sending messages from England? They already had a number of double agents working for them, but this García – he had achieved something remarkable. It was very important now that García reach Britain and continue what he started.

Of course, García was supposed to be already in England, so he couldn't just get the commercial plane from Lisbon to Whitchurch Airport – the Germans regularly checked the passenger lists. Instead he was sent to Gibraltar by ship and then flew from Gibraltar by air, on 24 April 1942, landing in Plymouth just after 5 p.m.

García does not identify the plane, but it was likely a Short Sunderland seaplane piloted by No. 10 Squadron of the Royal Australian Air Force. Their records from the base at Mount Batten declare that Aircraft W.3983 left Gibraltar at 0715 hours for a return flight to Mount Batten in Plymouth Harbour. It was an uneventful flight completed at 1705 hours – they were in the air for nearly ten hours, taking a circuitous route over the Atlantic to avoid any German aircraft. There were eight passengers on this flight, though García remembers only two passengers besides himself and it was apparently very uncomfortable. By the time he arrived in Plymouth, he was cold, very nervous and very hungry.

By April 1942, Plymouth had been decimated by the Luftwaffe, but the British Intelligence agents who met García at Mount Batten found him a hotel for the night while they arranged for his travel to London the following day. García's arrival was a national security secret – he would be known only by the code name Garbo. His chief contact, MI5 officer Tomás Harris, spoke fluent Spanish and would transform Agent Garbo into the finest double agent of the war.

Garbo/García would subsequently set up a false network of twenty-five German agents and Nazi sympathisers working in Britain, all reporting completely false information to the Germans via a non-existent commercial pilot flying between Whitchurch Airport and Lisbon.

On 1 June 1943, the Luftwaffe shot down Flight 777, killing all the Dutch crew and the passengers, including film star Leslie Howard (see Chapter 14). Garbo/García/Arabel complained bitterly to German Intelligence – he was furious at this interruption to his work. How were he and his agents supposed to do their jobs when their intelligence links were shot down by stupid German pilots! The lives of his network were in jeopardy, he declared – completely untrue, but German Intelligence informed the Luftwaffe who then held an investigation into the incident. Although the German crew who shot down Flight 777 were not reprimanded, it's interesting that there were no further attacks on the civilian airline between south-west England and Lisbon.

Meanwhile, these regular flights between Lisbon and England's south west were transporting more double agents and information to the British: Dusko Popov, Hungarian businessman, had first arrived in south-west England at Whitchurch Airport in December 1940, and subsequently made frequent trips to and from south-west England, feeding false information to the Germans; Ian Wilson of MI5 and Major Frank Foley of MI6 travelled into Portugal on 10 November 1943, under the respective pseudonyms 'Mr Watson' and 'Mr Fairclough', accompanying Dusko Popov on his visit to see his German 'masters', plying them with false information about D-Day; Lily Sergeyev, born in France though of Russian origin, had been smuggled into Britain via Whitchurch Airport, but betrayed the trust of the British authorities by planning to send false messages back to them and then, when she was in Lisbon prior to D-Day, by meeting her German 'handler'; and of course, García's false spies continued their work for the Germans. Apparently both a pilot and a steward of flights from south-west England and into Lisbon were working for German intelligence – both completely fake of course.

Throughout 1943 and 1944, Garbo's false network continued, the false lives of his agents reading like a script from a soap opera. His efforts successfully ensured that no real German spies ever got anywhere near the preparations for D-Day. García may have been a failure in real life, but his imagination would be the foundation of the Allies' success on 6 June 1944.

There are many excellent accounts of all the real double agents and their roles on D-Day, describing the brilliance of British Intelligence's Operation 'Double-Cross', but many of the accounts depict the German agents involved as stupid, easily taken in by García's lies.

In fact the head of the Abwehr overseeing the German Intelligence agents knew all about D-Day. He knew García's reports were false and he willingly and knowingly accepted the lies because the head of the Abwehr was happily telling Hitler exactly what Hitler wanted to hear.

WILHELM CANARIS

Wilhelm Canaris was a captain in the German Navy during the First World War. He was responsible for sinking the *Dresden* but, like any military officer, he had great respect for his enemy – and the Royal Navy admired Canaris both as a great captain and a master at military strategy.

As the First World War ended, Canaris found himself stranded in South America and on the run – he was very much a wanted man by the British military. Canaris spoke fluent Spanish so managed to obtain a passport and papers in Chile, and boarded a passenger ship heading for Plymouth, pretending that he was a Chilean citizen on his way to accept some inherited property in the Netherlands.

While on board the ship, Canaris made a particular effort to get to know the English passengers and their customs and by the end of the journey he was fluent in English.

On arrival in Plymouth in 1918, he was questioned by officers at Devonport. Some versions of this story say that the officials were suspicious of Canaris because his disguise was 'too perfect', but after happily submitting to their questions, and offering a great deal of information about his fellow English passengers, Canaris was free to go on his way to Europe. If he'd been detained, he would have proved a major catch.

Canaris then actively worked with Franco during the Spanish Civil War, and as a proud German officer he initially supported Hitler's rise to power. However, the plans for European domination and the attacks on the Jews soon convinced Canaris that Hitler was not only insane, but a danger to Germany and its people. Canaris was dismayed when the British prime minister, Neville Chamberlain, initially made peace with Hitler.

Canaris and his small secret group decided they must actively work towards Hitler's downfall from the inside. They knew an early assassination would just turn the Führer into a martyr to be replaced by yet another of his mad cronies, but they did what they could to save dozens of Jews from the concentration camps – even employing them as German spies so they could get to England. And suddenly an incredulous MI6 was receiving coded messages from the head of German Military Intelligence. They had an ally at Hitler's right hand.

When the Spanish chicken farmer Juan Pujol García first started sending false information via a German intermediary, it was received by Canaris' team with enthusiasm. García's information that Glaswegians enjoyed 'litres of wine' would have been accepted by many Germans, but Canaris had been in Plymouth; he knew the English drank their beer in pints not litres. And yet the false information was passed on to Hitler as 100 per cent accurate.

Here was the fatal flaw in Hitler's plans to defeat any Allied invasion – the head of his own military intelligence was actively working against him. Of course, not every German commander agreed with Hitler's belief that the Allied invasion would be at Calais. Generalfeldmarschall Erwin Rommel was fortifying Normandy and, believing the beaches there to be an ideal invasion point, asked for the Channel Islands' fortifications and guns to be moved there. Hitler said '*Nein*'. On 6 June 1944, the Allied Forces swept on past the Channel Islands, sailing around all those hard-built fortifications, and attacked the beaches at Normandy. Rommel had been right.

Just before D-Day, the Canaris team tried for one last time to assassinate Hitler. The Führer was due to meet with his High Command and Canaris and his team set a bomb in the meeting room. The meeting room was obliterated. However, Hitler had moved the meeting at the very last moment, and so Canaris' team were arrested and eventually executed in a most brutal fashion – hanged from coat hooks by piano wire. They died slowly in agony. Canaris was hanged twice, to extend the torture. This was one of the last of over twenty recorded attempts (by various groups and individuals) to assassinate Hitler. They started as early as 1934 and the final attempt came on 20 July 1944 by Claus von Stauffenberg.

A number of writers have stated that Canaris' imprisonment and execution was brilliant luck for the Allied invasion – the German Military Intelligence was decimated by the executions just at the right time. However, British Intelligence was dismayed. If Hitler didn't trust Canaris and his team, would Hitler now have the sense to review all the intelligence he'd received and realise he'd been fed false information? Would he realise that the Allied invasion wasn't coming via Calais after all?

Canaris' death could have been a major blow to the preparations for D-Day. Fortunately his replacement did not have the sense to review the intelligence and Hitler remained convinced that the 'little skirmish' going on in Normandy was just a ruse by the Allies to distract his attention from the full force heading for Calais. By the time Hitler realised his mistake, the Allied Forces were well on their way to victory.

If those Devonport officials had not let Canaris go in 1918, the D-Day landings of 1944 might well have been a very different story.

THE END OF
THE ROAD

In 2010, residents of Torquay's Lisburne Crescent were worried about the 'cat lady'. Eileen had not been seen for several days. They knew she was getting old – in fact she was 89 – and the weather was poor; perhaps she preferred to stay indoors. They would have knocked but the old dear didn't like to be disturbed – if you tried to make conversation with her in the street, she'd run away, though once in a while she would chat about her cat, the little ginger stray

Torquay, home of Eileen Nearne. (Library of Congress, LC-DIG-ppmsc-08907)

Torquay Pier and Harbour with the illuminations. (Author's collection)

she'd rescued. She was a recluse, a little unkempt at times, but that didn't stop them worrying about her absence and as the weather brightened, there was still no sign of her.

When the police broke in, they discovered Eileen Nearne had sadly died from a heart attack a few days before. They began the long search for relatives, rummaging through the piles of photos and letters in her flat. At long last they were able to make contact with her niece in Italy, who told them an extraordinary story.

Eileen Nearne was secretly a war hero. She had been a wireless operator in Paris working for the Special Operations Executive in 1944 when she was captured by the Gestapo and tortured. Hers was a terrifying story of survival.

Born in Britain but growing up in France, Eileen was the youngest of four children and nicknamed Didi. She idolised her older sister Jacqueline and the sisters had a special bond. So in 1942 when Jacqueline turned 26 and headed for Marseilles to find a way to England, Didi (just 21) had to go too. They were British citizens but finding a way from Marseilles to England was still impossible and eventually they had to get a train to Spain, then into Portugal where a ship took them to Gibraltar and another ship to Glasgow.

It took hours from there to get to London, where they sought in vain for work that might help the war effort – but they just weren't qualified for anything. One day Jacqueline received a message from a Captain Jepson, asking her to come in for an interview. Didi pestered her sister to ask if there was work for her too and a month later, there was another letter, this time for Didi.

The work was for the SOE, for the French section. They were desperately looking for men and women who could speak the language, to be trained to go back into France as secret agents.

Captain Jepson was a renowned talent spotter and he could see Jacqueline was just the kind of person they needed. In 1942, his bosses in SOE were uneasy about employing women, but Jepson believed women were better for this sort of undercover work than men. Didi he wasn't sure about – she seemed too young, perhaps not yet capable of coping on her own in occupied France, but she was enthusiastic and intelligent. Jepson employed her as a wireless operator to stay in England and receive the agents' messages from France.

Didi was disappointed. She wanted to go to France like her sister, but she would just have to wait. Jacqueline had to wait too – despite her training, Jacqueline's trainer's report declared that she was not very intelligent and lacked confidence. However, it was Colonel Buckmaster, head of SOE's French section, who made the final decision. Buckmaster admired beauty and Jacqueline was particularly beautiful, so she was declared 'one of the best we have had' on his report, and sent into France.

She was given the code name Jacqueline, which – as it was her real name – seemed to her pretty useless as cover, but she didn't question it. Jacqueline was then introduced to her new boss, Maurice Southgate, survivor of the *Lancastria*. After two years' training with SOE, he was eager to get back to France – he'd not seen his wife since 1940. Jacqueline would be acting as his only courier as they established the STATIONER network, which covered half of France from central Châteauroux to Tarbes in the south west.

But getting there was not going to be easy. The first plane got them over the dropping zone but there was no reception committee. The second saw only fog and turned back, as did the third. The fourth plane developed a technical problem and never left the runway. Finally in January 1943, they were heading for a blind parachute drop with no reception committee, but it was the best they could manage.

Jacqueline jumped first, into the dark. On landing safely, she gathered up her parachute but as she stood up, she saw the silhouette of a man pointing a gun at her, with two other figures beside him.

She was heartbroken to be caught so quickly, but then she heard her name whispered – the man turned out to be Southgate and the two others turned out to be tree stumps.

Nervously they set out to get the train to Clermont-Ferrand. On the way, they met a woman with a bicycle but Southgate instantly blew their cover by asking for directions in English. The woman looked at him bewildered and frightened, but Jacqueline repeated the question in French and the woman looked relieved. The woman couldn't speak English and had mistaken them for Germans.

Jacqueline had the details of their contact in Clermont-Ferrand, so when they finally arrived, she left Southgate at a café and headed off. She wasn't gone long, but to Southgate it seemed like a lifetime and he was relieved when she returned, believing something had happened to her.

Once settled in the home of the family Nerault, Jacqueline Nearne and Maurice Southgate quickly became two of the most successful agents working with the French Resistance. Their efforts running the STATIONER circuit were tireless; training the Resistance teams, arranging ammunition and supplies to be delivered by parachute, and doing a little sabotage of their own.

During 1943, the STATIONER circuit achieved an impressive list of successful missions. In just a few months they destroyed: the generators at the aircraft engine factory in Limoges; an electricity sub-station in Bezac along with twenty-seven trucks bound for Germany; pylons at Dun-le-Poëlier, Vierzon and Pau; arsenals at Tulle and Tarbes; loading cranes at Brive-la-Gaillarde and Tulle; pumps at the steel mill in Ancizes; the transformers at the Hispano–Suiza airplane engine factory in Tarbes; and the aluminium plant in Lannemezan by cutting off the electricity, leaving the aluminium to solidify. They also destroyed rail-lines and signals and stole 30,000 litres of German petrol in Saignes. The year 1944 would prove to be more of the same.

Very soon Maurice Southgate's code name 'Hector' was notorious and despised by the Germans. As D-Day approached, it was Southgate who finally managed to get the leaders of the Resistance forces to form a co-ordinating body, ready for a maximum offensive to disrupt the German Forces as the Allies landed on 6 June 1944. Special Operations Executive established the Jedburgs, a body of agents specifically trained to ready the Resistance for D-Day, parachuting them in during 1944, working with the French Resistance circuits and preparing the 'ground' as it were for the Allied offensive. While the Allied Forces attacked on the Normandy beaches – with over 160,000 men, the largest amphibious attack in world history – thousands of the French Resistance would be making things as difficult as possible 'behind the lines' so the Germans were less able to defend themselves.

But Southgate would not see D-Day.

DIDI IN PARIS

Meanwhile, Jacqueline's sister Didi had got what she wanted. At last, in 1944, she was parachuted into France to send wireless messages from Paris, although her sister Jacqueline would never know she was there. Jacqueline had requested that Didi not be sent into the field – she was worried about her – but Didi's persistence and SOE's desperate need for wireless operators meant that Didi eventually had her way.

Jacqueline became ill. The work they'd achieved had worn her out and, in April 1944, she was sent home to recover, collected by a Lysander aircraft from a field a few kilometres north of Châteauroux. Also boarding the plane was Southgate's wife Josette, who'd stayed in Paris throughout the war and from 1943 supported her husband's work for the Resistance, giving the STATIONER circuit 200,000 francs – all the money she had. She would eventually get the money back in London, to help with her living expenses there. With the Germans closing in on her husband 'Hector', Josette had to be evacuated, but would she ever see her husband again?

Also boarding the plane was Agent Regis, real name Jean Savy, from the WIZARD circuit. Unknown to Jacqueline, Regis was Didi's boss. Regis had discovered that the Germans were developing a long-range rocket (the V1) capable of carrying a 1.25-ton warhead, with the potential to destroy large areas of London and cities in the south east of England. The RAF had hit the experimental V1 rocket site the year before, but production had recovered and thousands of V1s were now ready to launch. Regis had to get to London personally with this sensitive information, leaving Didi alone in Paris.

Didi was transferred to a new circuit called SPIRITUALIST, still in Paris. She enjoyed the work, despite the isolation. By mid-July 1944, she had sent 105 messages and had worked alone in secret for four months. This was longer than was safe to stay in one location, so she prepared to set up a new location on the other side of Paris.

On 21 July, she prepared to make her last transmission from the 'old' location, but there was a power-cut, so she stayed there to sleep.

When she awoke, the power was back on, so she reassembled her wireless transmitter and checked the aerial. Just as she was finishing her transmission, she heard a car engine outside, followed by shouting in the street and car doors banging. She wiped the condensation from the window to see, to her horror, that the Germans had found her, using a direction-finding vehicle.

It would be moments before the Germans were knocking down her door.

Didi frantically dismantled the transmitter and the aerial, hiding the pieces in a cupboard. The papers including her codes she managed to burn in the oven, but it took so long there was no time to save herself.

But Didi had an incredible ability for play-acting.

As the first German pushed his way into the apartment, gun in hand, he was surprised to be accosted by some angry girl demanding to know what he was doing. She didn't seem very bright. He informed her that he was searching for someone sending messages on an illegal wireless set.

'Wireless set?' the girl looked amazed. 'Isn't that something you listen to? How can you send messages on a wireless?'

The plain-clothed German looked dumbfounded.

'If you tell me what it looks like,' the girl suggested, 'perhaps I can help you search for it.'

The German hesitated, taking a step back towards the door. Didi's assured performance had nearly fooled him. But instead he called for his men to ransack the apartment and soon the pieces of the wireless set were thrown in her face.

The Gestapo had sent seventeen German agents to find this enemy wireless operator and they were determined to take whoever they found at the apartment in for questioning. At Gestapo headquarters, Didi maintained her performance as a simple-minded country girl called Jacqueline du Tertre, working for some (non-existent) man who paid her to send some funny messages for him. Her interrogators were utterly confused.

Even when they smacked her across the face, she refused to be intimidated. Now she was an outraged country girl called Jacqueline du Tertre. Questioned for hours, she never broke character. Even when faced with torture by *baignoire*, she remained Jacqueline du Tertre. She was plunged into an ice-cold bath, head held under until she struggled for breath and her mouth and nose filled with water. Just as she thought she would die, they lifted her out, asked her a question, and pushed her back under. As her body went limp, they brought her back up, but still they could not get the answers they were seeking. As she spewed water over herself and the interrogators, she could hear angry voices in the background – she had frustrated them and that made her feel triumphant.

She had given them nothing but non-existent names and false addresses. For all they knew, Didi really was Jacqueline du Tertre; her performance had succeeded and they had failed to break her, but that didn't stop the Germans sending her first to the horrors of Ravensbrück and then, in February 1945, to Buchenwald concentration camp.

THE END FOR MAURICE SOUTHGATE

In April 1944, Southgate's STATIONER network, now comprising over 2,500 men and women, was preparing for D-Day. Several arrests in Châteauroux made staying there dangerous – Southgate, as Agent Hector, had a price on his head. So, along with his assistant René Maingard (who had arrived with Henry Rée the year before), he decided to move the whole operation to Montluçon until the furore died down.

Once in Montluçon, Maingard went to sort out the messages while Southgate visited the house of his new wireless operator Réné Mathieu. Meanwhile, Southgate's Resistance allies were desperately trying to reach him at the train station to tell him the Gestapo had set a trap for Hector at Mathieu's house. They were too late.

Southgate arrived at the Rue de Rimard. He was exhausted. He had a lot on his mind. On a normal day, he might have spotted the secret police wandering up and down the street, trying and possibly failing to look inconspicuous – Southgate had always been security minded, he was considered one of SOE's best agents. But today of all days he knocked on Mathieu's door without making any security checks.

The door flew open and Southgate was caught by the Gestapo.

At Gestapo headquarters he was beaten and handcuffed by young French thugs now working for the Gestapo. They took great delight in humiliating him. They stole everything he had – his watch, his wallet – but he had nothing incriminating on him. They didn't yet know just who they had caught.

Not until he was transferred for interrogation to the infamous headquarters of the Sicherheitsdienst, the branch of the Gestapo dealing specifically with counter-espionage, did Southgate realise they had discovered he was Hector, organiser of the STATIONER circuit. Someone he knew had 'shopped' him, but fortunately there had been time for his team to get away. That was some consolation for him to grasp hold of while he suffered weeks of interrogation and atrocious conditions in the prison cells.

Then just after D-Day, a few months before the liberation of Paris, Maurice Southgate and thirty-six other SOE agents were sent to Buchenwald concentration camp. On 16 September 1944, sixteen of these SOE agents were hanged. Southgate faked a stomach cramp and, through the intervention of another SOE agent, he was admitted to the camp hospital (oddly the Germans would not hang him while he was ill). Soon, though, the fake illness became a real illness and after several weeks slowly recovering in the hospital, Southgate was assigned to a tailor's workshop onsite. There he witnessed the horror of the concentration camps, with tattooed human skin hanging up to dry. He kept a low profile, frantically finding hiding places in the camp with other surviving SOE agents when the SS began hunting them down …

LIBERATION

D-Day. And Lucien Dumais and the Shelburne Line team were still hard at work. They'd managed to steal 150 fugitives through German lines and were heading for the coast. But as the Allied

D-Day: Mulberry Harbour at Cherbourg. (Library of Congress, LC-W33-56551-ZC)

Normandy invasion, June 1944. A convoy of landing craft sails across
the English Channel toward the Normandy Invasion beaches on D-Day,
6 June 1944. Each of these landing craft is towing a barrage balloon for
protection against low-flying German aircraft. (Photography from the US
Coast Guard Collection in the US National Archives. Photo # 26-G-2333)

trucks thundered past them on the road, collecting men and
munitions from the French ports, could Dumais get anyone to
help the downed airmen get back to England? It was impossible,
he informed Airey Neave and Jimmy Langley anxiously waiting
for them in London, escape lines across the Channel were finished, and his job was over – the war was literally heading in the
opposite direction.

The Allies were coming, but it seemed too late for Georges Jouanjean,
the Pat Line recruit who'd rescued Gordon Carter. The Germans
had taken the remaining prisoners from Flossenburg concentration
camp and force-marched them 400 miles across southern Germany.
Thousands of the prisoners died en route, and many killed themselves rather than go on.

Prisoner at a concentration camp at Flossenburg. (Library of Congress, LC-USZ62-128309)

But suddenly there was the deafening roar of tanks. Georges turned to see the Americans had caught up with them. At last, he was free.

Gordon Carter was also on a forced march, in a column of British prisoners of war being herded north by desperate German guards towards the River Elbe and the Baltic Sea. Berlin had fallen to the Russians, but thankfully the Cheshire Regiment turned up at last to free the British prisoners.

Less than a month later, Janine Jouanjean was at her grandparents' house when she looked through the window to see a car pull up outside and an RAF officer step out, in full uniform. Could this be the scruffy airman she'd not seen for two and a half years? Twenty-three days later, she and Gordon Carter were married. By some miracle, all of Janine's family had survived and even her brother Georges returned home, looking unwell but safe and in time for the wedding celebrations. It was a wonderful ceremony.

The skinny Nazi girl was complaining again to the American officer. His soldiers, she said, were giving cigarettes to the Nazi prisoners, treating the Germans much better than they'd treated the concentration camp victims.

There was definitely something odd about this 'Nazi girl', so the Americans interrogated her again, but still they didn't believe her story; there were too many details she couldn't remember. She declared she was Eileen Nearne, an SOE agent, but couldn't remember her agent's number or the name of her contact in Paris. She said she'd been interrogated by the Germans but hadn't given them any information – the Americans were incredulous at that – and then she'd been sent to Ravensbrück and Buchenwald before she'd finally managed to escape from a forced march.

Throughout the torture and the starvation, Eileen Nearne (Didi) had maintained her false identity as a French girl called Jacqueline du Tertre. Now, when she was desperately trying to prove to the Allies who she really was, they didn't believe her. The US officer in charge of the Master Interrogation Center declared, 'She often is unable to answer even the simplest questions, as though she were impersonating someone else.'

Mental health problems would plague Eileen Nearne for the rest of her life, unsurprising considering the nightmares she'd experienced, though to her niece and friends she was always kind, funny and a tireless charity worker. In 1993, Eileen Nearne bravely returned to Ravensbrück to attend a memorial ceremony. Many of her SOE friends and others she met in the camps stayed in contact. The Torquay flat was full of letters from them.

After the war, Eileen's sister Jacqueline worked for the United Nations and sadly died in 1982, aged 66. Her SOE colleague

Harry Rée delivered the eulogy, warmly describing Jacqueline's stoicism and her magnetic personality.

In 2010, hundreds gathered in Torquay for the funeral of Eileen Nearne; Didi's coffin was draped with British and French flags as Scottish pipers escorted the *cortège* to the church. She'd lived an incredible life and left behind a flat full of astonishing stories.

Just four of the SOE agents imprisoned at Buchenwald lived to see its liberation by American Forces on 11 April 1945. Among them was Maurice Southgate; the survivor of the *Lancastria* sinking in 1940 had survived Buchenwald concentration camp. Southgate eventually returned to Paris after the war to work with his wife again, designing furniture. He suffered poor health for the rest of his life but he had survived. As Maurice Southgate sat in the chair at the American War Crimes Trials held at Dachau in 1947, he described to them all of the horrors, the hangings, the drying human skins with their poignant tattoos.

It had been a hell of a war.

TIMELINE OF THE SECOND WORLD WAR

These are the dates relevant to *South West Secret Agents*. If you are looking for a more detailed timeline, I highly recommend:

www.spartacus.schoolnet.co.uk/2WWchron.htm

For detailed timelines of Operation Aerial, which illustrate the full extent, dangers and the chaos of the evacuation and related battles, have a look at these websites:

www.naval-history.net/xDKWDa-Aerial.htm
www.naval-history.net/xDKWW2-4006-19JUN03.htm

15 March 1939	German Army invades Czechoslovakia
23 August 1939	The USSR and Germany sign the Nazi-Soviet Pact
1 September 1939	German Army invades Poland
3 September 1939	Britain and France declare war on Germany
	UK Parliament passes the National Services (Armed Forces) Act
	Winston Churchill appointed First Lord of the Admiralty
12 March 1940	Paul Reynaud replaces Édouard Daladier as prime minister of France
10 May 1940	Germany invades France, the Western offensive begins

10 May 1940	Neville Chamberlain resigns as UK prime minister, replaced by Winston Churchill
14 May 1940	Formation of the UK Local Defence Forces (later renamed Home Guard)
27 May 1940	Evacuation begins from Dunkirk
28 May 1940	Belgium surrenders
4 June 1940	Last of the evacuation from Dunkirk (338,000 British, French and Belgian Forces)
17 June 1940	Henri-Philippe Pétain replaces Paul Reynaud as prime minister of France and begins negotiations with Germany
22 June 1940	Pétain's government signs the armistice with Germany, dividing France into two zones and creating 'Vichy France'
28 June 1940	Winston Churchill recognises Charles de Gaulle as leader of the Free French Forces in exile, based in London
3 July 1940	Threatened with attack, the Royal Navy destroys most of the French Navy at Mers-el-Kebir
6 July 1940	First bomb hits Plymouth
10 July 1940	The Battle of Britain begins
11 July 1940	Henri-Philippe Pétain appointed president of Vichy France
16 July 1940	Hugh Dalton establishes the Special Operations Executive (SOE)
12 October 1940	Adolf Hitler postpones the invasion of Britain
23 October 1940	Adolf Hitler meets Francisco Franco to persuade Spain to join the war against the Allies
12 July 1941	Soviet Union and Britain sign an agreement of mutual aid
7 December 1941	Japanese Forces attack Pearl Harbour, bringing the USA into the war
27 March 1942	Allied raid on St Nazaire
23 April 1942	Luftwaffe start bombing historic cities in Britain, including Exeter and Bath, known as the Baedeker Bombings
19 August 1942	The attempted landings at Dieppe, known at the Battle of Dieppe
11 November 1942	Adolf Hitler orders the occupation of Vichy France

8 July 1943	Jean Moulin, leader of the French Resistance, murdered by Gestapo
22 March 1944	Pierre Brossolette, one of the leaders of the French Resistance, murdered by Gestapo
6 June 1944	D-Day, Allied landings on the beaches of Normandy
20 July 1944	'July Plot' to assassinate Hitler fails
10 September 1944	French provisional government abolishes Vichy legislature
11 September 1944	Allied troops enter Nazi Germany
4 February 1945	Winston Churchill, Joseph Stalin and Franklin D. Roosevelt meet at the Yalta Conference
25 April 1945	Liberation of Dachau concentration camp
4 May 1945	All military forces in Germany surrender to the Allies
8 May 1945	Winston Church announces Victory in Europe (VE) Day
28 May 1945	William Joyce (Lord Haw Haw) captured

NOTES AND FURTHER ACKNOWLEDGEMENTS

I love a good spy story, and as I was reading about British espionage in the Second World War, I encountered the same phrase over and over: 'When I got back to England …' Whether the agent was in France or Gibraltar or Eastern Europe or North Africa, that same phrase kept coming up, and I thought to myself, 'The English Channel is a very wide expanse of water and very dangerous, not only because of the weather but because travellers were under constant threat of attack by the Germans during the Second World War. How on earth did all these people – tens of thousands of them – get safely back to England?' But every spy story I read seemed to end with the agent on a beach or at a port somewhere, and their next sentence would start 'When I got back to England …' or sometimes 'On my return to London …' which is even more difficult considering the lack of available transport in wartime. So I started researching these journeys and discovered that the south west of England where I live was a maelstrom of clandestine activity during the Second World War, and so this book was born.

Of course I knew about the bombings and the Blitz, the destruction of Plymouth, Exeter and the attacks on Dartmouth, and the gathering of so many troops ready for D-Day, but I never realised just how many people in the south west were doing so much more than just surviving the attacks; they were fighting back in ways that only an area steeped in the history of smuggling can even imagine.

The idea that these agents, both in the south west and in western Europe, 'did their bit' is an understatement – yes, they did their duty, but with imagination, courage and an audacity that I find incredible. At a time when everyone was struggling, when defeat sometimes seemed inevitable, they made the very best of what they had available to them and forged a series of retaliatory strikes against overwhelming odds, continuing over many years, that refused to let the Germans believe they had won anything. For these people, the skirmishes and rescues were not going to end until the Nazis were ultimately defeated.

I hope that this book helps to make readers aware of the actions of their fellow countrymen in south-west England during the Second World War. There are still so many more stories out there so check out the excellent books in the references section. There were so many websites I could recommend that I thought it best to list them as links on my website: www.lauraquigley.weebly.com.

I have listed the agents' relatives at the front of the book as they deserve a special thanks. While collecting these stories, many others also helped me along and they too deserve a big thank you: Cate Ludlow and her excellent team at The History Press, including Chris West for the excellent cover and editor Ruth Boyes who meticulously corrected my many mistakes and clarified the details. Also Hidden Heritage; Polperro News for offering such wonderful photographs; Scott Grenney and his Eddystone Media website team at www.BarbicanWaterfront.com; the Old Plymouth Society; and the Plymouth Historical Association for their continuing support. I hope all my friends on the Facebook pages enjoy this latest effort – it's always lovely hearing from you.

A LIST OF
THE AGENTS

And of course, my final thanks must go to the agents themselves for living these stories (in alphabetic order with aliases and relevant chapters indicated):

G.W. Abbott (10)
Jack Alcock (14)
Francis Basin (9)
Albert Bedane (10)
John Bell (2)
David Birkin (8 and 10)
Ivan Black (10)
Raymond Le Bosse (13)
Maurice Buckmaster (17)
Marie-Thérèse Le Calvec (13)
Wilhelm Canaris (16)
Mathilde Carré ('La Chatte', 10)
Gordon Carter (12 and 17)
Madame Collai (11)
François Le Cornec (13)
Raymond Le Corre (3, 7 and 8)
Ben Cowburn (10)
Norman Crockett (11)
John Dingley (5)
Georges Dubourdin (9)
Doctor Le Duc (10)

Lucien Dumais (11, 13 and 17)
William Dunderdale (8)
Stuart Edmundson (5)
William Falcon (5)
Juan Pujol García (16)
John Garnet (9)
Lucien Germereau
 ('Lucien Pradier', 14)
Jean-Jacques Gilbert
 ('JJ Tremayne'/'JJ Allen', 9)
Tom Greene (8)
Colin Gubbins (5 and 8)
Jacques Guéguen (8)
Guillaume Le Guen (8)
Albert-Marie Guérisse
 ('Pat O'Leary', 9, 11 and 12)
Pierre Guillet (8 and 10)
Charles Harris (2)
Jean Hauger ('Agent Macout', 15)
Pierre Hentic ('Agent Maho', 8)
Norman Hope (2)

Leslie Howard (14 and 16)
Pip Jarvis (8 and 9)
Selwyn Jepson (17)
Andrée de Jongh (11)
Georges Jouanjean (12 and 17)
Janine Jouanjean (12 and 17)
Marian Kadulski ('Krajewski', 11)
Jimmy Langley (1, 11, 12, 13 and 17)
Jasper Lawn (9)
Robert Leroy (9)
Daniel Lomenech (9)
Tom Long (8)
Len Macey (8)
Steven Mackenzie (9)
René Maingard (15 and 17)
Louis Marec (12)
Doctor de la Marnière (8)
Philip Martel (10)
Réné Mathieu (17)
François Mitterrand (10)
Conchita Montenegro (14)
Hubert Moreau (3, 7 and 8)
Desmond Mulholland (10)
Cookie Nash (9)
Eileen Nearne ('Didi', 17)
Jacqueline Nearne (17)

Airey Neave (11, 13 and 17)
John Newton (8 and 10)
Hubert Nicolle (10)
Bernard Nowell (2)
Paul O'Brien (9)
G.C.B. Redding (10)
Harry Rée (15)
Gilbert Renault ('Rémy',
    9 and 10)
Howard Rendle (8)
Brook Richards (8)
Raymond Roche (9)
Josette Ronserail (14)
Ernest Sibiril (8)
Jean Savy ('Regis', 17)
Jean Simon (15)
Maurice Southgate (1, 2, 15 and 17)
James Symes (10)
Claude Antoinette Thierry-Mieg (14)
Richard Townsend (9)
K.M. Uhr-Henry (8)
Bevil Warington Smyth (8)
Nigel Warington Smyth (8)
Cyril Wellington (5)
Herbert Wellington (5)

REFERENCES

Addison, Paul and Crang, Jeremy A. (eds), *Listening to Britain* (The Bodley Head, 2010).

Aitkin, Nicholas, *The Forgotten French: Exiles in the British Isles 1940–44* (Manchester University Press, 2003).

Baff, Flight Lieutenant K.C., *Maritime is Number Ten – The Sunderland Era: A History of No. 10 Squadron RAAF* (Griffin Press, 1983).

Bailey, Roderick, *Forgotten Voices of the Secret War* (Ebury Press in association with the Imperial War Museum, 2009).

Bassett, Richard, *Hitler's Spy Chief – The Wilhelm Canaris Mystery* (Phoenix, 2011).

Bazin, Nancy, *Women at War* (Fountain, 2002).

Beevor, Antony, *D-Day* (Viking, 2009).

Beevor, Antony, *The Second World War* (Phoenix, 2013).

Boyce, F. and Everett, D., *SOE: The Scientific Secrets* (Sutton Publishing, 2003).

Bracken, C.W., *A History of Plymouth* (S.R. Publishers Ltd, 1931).

Breuer, William B., *Daring Missions of World War II* (John Wiley & Sons Inc., 2001).

Breuer, William B., *The Spy Who Spent the War in Bed* (John Wiley & Sons Inc., 2003).

Brown, Ashley, *Dunkirk and the Great Western* (Great Western Railway Company, not dated).

Buckton, Henry, *Devon at War Through Time* (Amberley, 2012).

Bunting, Madeleine, *The Model Occupation: The Channel Islands Under German Rule 1940–1945* (Pimlico, 2004 edition).

Cardigan, Chandos Sydney Cedric Brudenell-Bruce, Earl of, *I Walked Alone* (Readers Union and Routledge and Kegan Paul, 1952).

Clamp, Arthur L., *Preparing for D-Day – American Assault Exercises at Slapton Sands, 1944* (Orchard Publications, Revised edition 2006).

Colvin, Ian, *Flight 777: The Mystery of Leslie Howard* (Pen and Sword, 2013 reprint of a 1957 publication).

Cookridge, E.H., *Set Europe Ablaze* (Pan Books, 1966, American edition 1969).

Dumais, Lucien, *The Man Who Went Back* (Futura Publications Ltd, 1975 edition).

Foot, M.R.D. and Langley, J.M., *MI9 Escape and Evasion 1939–1945* (Book Club Associates, 1979).

Fountain, Nigel (consulting editor) *Women at War* (Imperial War Museum Sound Archive, Michael O'Mara Books, 2002).

Freeman, Ray (ed.), *A Wrens-Eye View of Wartime Dartmouth* (Dartmouth History Research Group, paper 12, 1994).

García, Juan Pujol and West, Nigel, *Operation Garbo* (Biteback Publishing, 2011, first published 1985).

Gill, Crispin, *Plymouth: A New History* (Devon Books, 1993).

Gray, Todd, *Blackshirts in Devon* (The Mint Press, 2006).

Hawkes, John, *Mount Batten Headland: History and Archaeology* (Plymouth City Museum and Art Gallery, 1998).

Hazell, Martin, *Poles Apart: Polish Naval Memories of World War Two, A Social History* (Southwest Maritime History Society, Maritime Monograph 6, Edition 2, 2012).

Hentic, Pierre, *Agent de L'ombre: Memoires 1941–1945* (Editions de la Martinière, 2012).

Hesketh, Robert, *Plymouth, a Shortish Guide* (Bossiney Books, 2010).

Higgins, Tony, *The Free French in Kingswear* (Dartmouth History Research Group paper 6, 1992).

Hunter, W.J., *From Coastal Command to Captivity* (Leo Cooper, 2003).

Lampe, David, *The Last Ditch: Britain's Secret Resistance and the Nazi Invasion Plans* (Frontline Books, 1968–2013 reprint).

Levine, Joshua, *Operation Fortitude* (Collins, 2011, 2012 reprint).

Macintyre, Ben, *Double Cross* (Bloomsbury, 2012).

Miller, Russell, *Behind the Lines* (Pimlico, 2003).

Murphy, Sean, *Letting the Side Down* (Sutton Publishing, 2003).

Nichol, John and Rennell, Tony, *Home Run: Escape from Nazi Europe* (Viking, 2007 and Penguin Books, 2008).

Ollier, Edmund, *Cassell's History of the United States* (Cassell, Petter & Galpin, 1874).

Ottaway, Susan, *Sisters, Secrets and Sacrifice* (Harper, 2013).

Pitchfork, Air Commodore Graham, *Shot Down and On the Run* (The National Archives, 2003).

Porter, Peter G., *Frank Jones and the Secret War: The Cross-Channel Exploits of the Coastal Command in World War 2* (CreateSpace Independent Publishing Platform, 2009).

Powell, Barry, *Devon's Glorious Past 1939–1945* (Two Hoots Publishing, 1995).

Richards, Brook, *Secret Flotillas Volume 1* (Pen and Sword Books Ltd, 2004, reprint, 2012).

Sarkar, Dilip, *How the Spitfire Won the Battle of Britain* (Amberley, 2010).

Scrivener, Keith, *Plymouth At War: A Pictorial Account 1939–1945* (Archive Publications Ltd, 1989).

Smith, Graham, *Devon and Cornwall Airfields in the Second World War* (Countryside Books, 2000).

Stafford, David, *Secret Agent: The True Story of the Special Operations Executive* (BBC, 2000).

Taylor, A.J.F., *English History 1914–1945* (Clarendon Press, 1965).

Tiersky, Ronald, *François Mitterrand: The Last French President* (St Martin's Press, 2000).

Twyford, H.P., *It Came To Our Door* (Pen and Ink Publishing, reprint of a 1945 publication, revised by Chris Robinson in 2005).

Warwicker, John, *Churchill's Underground Army* (Frontline Books, 2008).

Wasley, Gerald, *Blitz: An Account of Hitler's Aerial War Over Plymouth in March 1941 and the Events That Followed* (Devon Books, 1991).

Wasley, Gerald, *Devon At War 1939–1945* (Devon Books, 1994).

Wasley, Gerald, *Mount Batten: The Flying Boats of Plymouth* (Halsgrove House, 2006).

Wise, James E., Jr and Baron, Scott, *Soldiers Lost at Sea: A Chronicle of Troopship Disasters* (Naval Institute Press, 2003).

For internet and video resources, please see
www.lauraquigley.weebly.com.

INDEX

For the list of agents, see pages 184 and 185

Also from The History Press

GREAT WAR BRITAIN

Great War Britain is a unique new local series to mark the centenary of the Great War. In partnership with archives and museums across Great Britain, the series provides an evocative portrayal of life during this 'war to end all wars'. In a scrapbook style, and beautifully illustrated, it includes features such as personal memoirs, letters home, diary extracts, newspaper reports, photographs, postcards and other local First World War ephemera.

Lightning Source UK Ltd.
Milton Keynes UK
UKOW07f0510140115

244458UK00007B/128/P